Camping
Georgia

Help Us Keep This Guide Up to Date

Every effort has been made by the author and editors to make this guide as accurate and useful as possible. However, many things can change after a guide is published—trails are rerouted, regulations change, techniques evolve, facilities come under new management, and so on.

We would love to hear from you concerning your experiences with this guide and how you feel it could be improved and kept up to date. While we may not be able to respond to all comments and suggestions, we'll take them to heart and we'll also make certain to share them with the author. Please send your comments and suggestions to the following address:

The Globe Pequot Press
Reader Response/Editorial Department
P.O. Box 480
Guilford, CT 06437

Or you may e-mail us at: editorial@globe-pequot.com

Thanks for your input, and happy travels!

Camping Georgia

Alex Nutt

FALCON®

GUILFORD, CONNECTICUT
HELENA, MONTANA

AN IMPRINT OF THE GLOBE PEQUOT PRESS

AFALCONGUIDE ®

Library of Congress Cataloging-in-Publication Data
Nutt, Alex.
   Camping Georgia / Alex Nutt.—1st ed.
     p. cm. — (A Falcon guide)
   Includes a bibliographical references and index.
   ISBN 0-7627-1077-2
   1. Camp sites, facilities, etc.—Georgia—Guidebooks. 2. Camping—Georgia—
Guidebooks. 3. Georgia—Guidebooks. I. Title. II. Series.

GV191.42.G4 N88 2002
796.54'09748—dc21   2002069302

Manufactured in the United States of America
First Edition/First Printing

This book would not have been nearly as much fun without my wife, coresearcher, and chief motivator, Kim, and our family camping crew—Stephanie, Trace, and AJ—along to make things more fun. They are constantly reminding me what's really important in life: being with family and enjoying the world around us.

Acknowledgments

The professionalism and integrity of the agencies that operate campgrounds in Georgia play a major role in making them such enjoyable destinations. Without fail, our experiences with these agencies—and the people that are their lifeblood—were positive ones. It takes a pretty special person to devote some or all of a career to making such experiences available to the general public. Tell them you appreciate them next time you go camping.

These agencies have also made a tremendous effort to make campgrounds and outdoor sites much more accessible for those with physical disabilities. Until you've walked a trail with a sightless person, you haven't really "seen" that trail completely. Until you've pushed a wheelchair along a paved forest trail, you haven't appreciated the basic act of walking freely. The outdoors should be as accessible to those with disabilities as is practical, and I applaud the efforts of the various agencies for their work in this area.

Most of these facilities could not operate without the able assistance of many volunteers, including the campground hosts. Next time you're enjoying yourself at one of these campgrounds, be sure to tell the volunteers how much you appreciate their help and dedication.

To the Georgia Department of Natural Resources, Parks and Historic Sights Division; the U.S.D.A. Forest Service; the U.S. Army Corps of Engineers; Georgia Power Company; and the various city and county government agencies that own and operate such facilities—thanks.

Contents

Map Legend

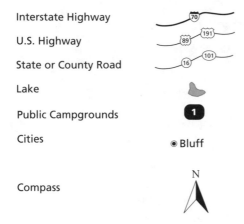

Interstate Highway	70
U.S. Highway	89 191
State or County Road	16 101
Lake	
Public Campgrounds	1
Cities	● Bluff
Compass	N

Key to Abbreviations

Y, yes; **N,** no

Hookups: W, water; E, electricity; S, sewer

Toilets: F, flush; V, vault

Recreation: B, boating; F, fishing; G, golf; H, hiking; L, boat launch; M, mountain biking; O, off-road vehicles; R, horseback riding; S, swimming; T, tennis

Fee: $, less than $10; $$, $10–$15; $$$, $16–$20; $$$$, more than $20

Maximum RV limit is given in feet.

Stay limit is given in days.

If no entry under **Season,** campground is open all year.

If no entry **Fee,** campground is free.

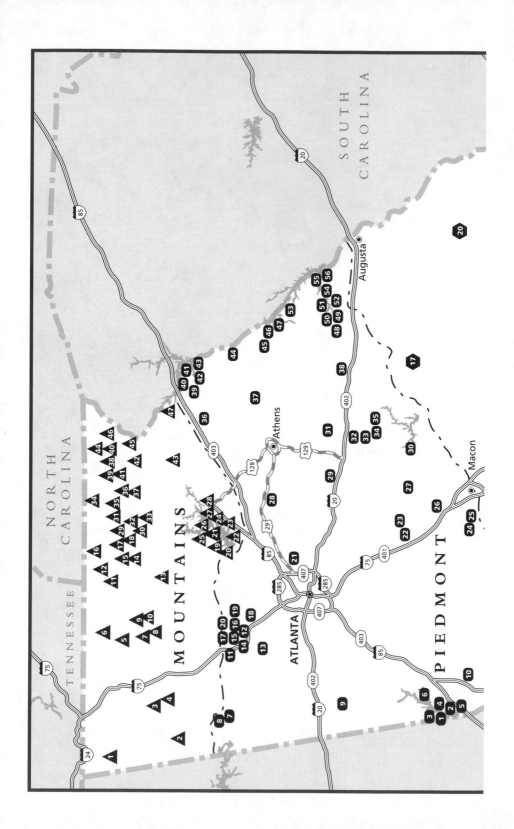

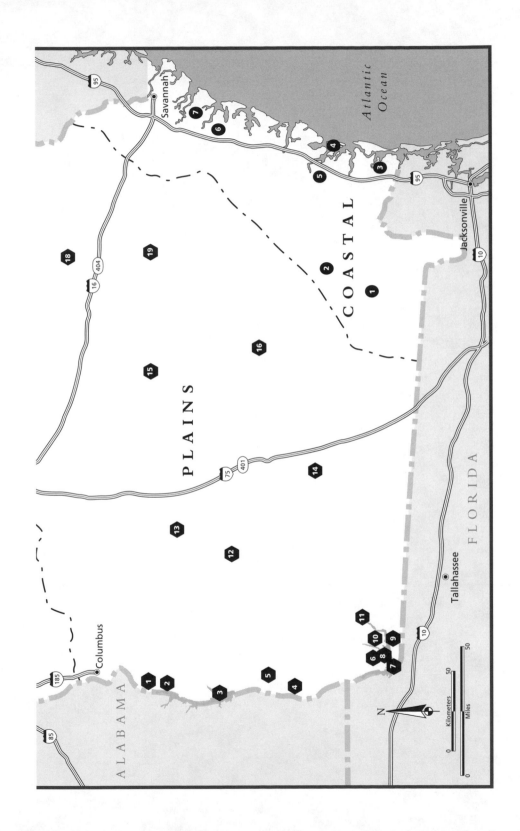

Introduction

Introduction to Georgia

Georgia is the largest state east of the Mississippi River, covering an area of more than 58,000 square miles. Georgia currently ranks tenth nationally in population, with more than 8 million. The state is a grand mixture of the old and the new. The modern, bustling city of Atlanta is home to several Fortune 500 companies and is a regional and national communications center. Atlanta and its surrounding communities have experienced continued rapid growth over the past 30 years, and the metro area now comprises many hundreds of square miles. Augusta, Savannah, Macon, Columbus, Athens, and Rome are some of the other larger urban areas around the state. Augusta and Savannah are two of the state's oldest cities, both having played parts in and retaining some history of the Revolutionary War, and later the Civil War. One of the greatest things about the state is the variety of people and cultures that one finds with just a little exploration. From the streets of the cities to the fields of the countryside is not that great a distance in miles or culture. Georgia's people are just as diverse and varied. When you visit, take some time to get to know the locals; you'll usually be rewarded with some great company.

Camping in Georgia

Georgia has a surprising wealth and diversity of quality public campgrounds. Many campgrounds offer a combination of different types of sites, including walk-in sites, tent sites, smaller trailer sites, and full pull-through sites. These combinations allow for a broad range of campers to enjoy the pleasures of quality camping. Most of Georgia's public campgrounds are located at or near some place of significance or interest--sometimes historical, sometimes topographical, and sometimes both. Those points of interest provide for entertainment and exploration while staying in the park and give you the opportunity to leave with a heightened sense of the history of the state and its people. Other campgrounds are located specifically to take advantage of a recreational opportunity (usually lakes and rivers). These areas offer a combination of the normal fun of camping combined with water sports, fishing, hunting, etc.

Georgia's weather is relatively mild throughout the year, and camping is a year-round sport in the middle and southern parts of the state. Caution is needed in the mountains, where the weather is more extreme and less predictable, and you'll find less camping activity in the winter. Check with the campground manager if you have any concerns. While most of Georgia's state parks are open all year, some Forest Service campgrounds close seasonally, and the Corps of Engineers campgrounds and Georgia Power Company campgrounds surrounding the larger lakes usually close in the winter as well. Winter camping in Georgia can offer an interesting new twist to an already fun activity--if you're properly prepared. If you prefer to stay away from the crowds, then the off-season is your best bet.

Which campground is best for your trip? That depends on what you're looking for. If you prefer to be as isolated from civilization and "close to nature," try one of the Forest Service campgrounds. They offer less in the way of utilities and worldly comforts at the tent site, and are less accommodating for larger RVs and trailers, but the locations and surroundings are well worth the trade-off.

Do you like water, boating, fishing, skiing, and sand beaches? Try the Corps of Engineers campgrounds around many of the lakes. They offer most amenities and can accommodate most larger RVs. The Georgia Power Company campgrounds are also located on lakes and offer most of the same comforts.

Want a little more history and local color? Then visit one of the state parks. You'll find one near you, wherever you are in the state, and they can accommodate most larger RVs. They also are the most diverse, so you're likely to find a little of everything.

Do you camp with kids? Most of the state park campgrounds are well suited for families, and some even have several of their campsites arranged around a play-ground so that parents can watch the kiddies and still relax a little themselves.

The best thing about camping in Georgia is that no matter where you go, you're sure to find just what you're looking for. And some of the best experiences and memories come from the unexpected discoveries that result from exploring the many options along the way.

How to Use This Book

Take this book; add some basic camping equipment, a little precaution, and lots of enthusiasm; and go camping! *Camping Georgia* includes listings of publicly operat-ed campgrounds accessible by either car or RV. Upon seeing a favorable weather forecast for the weekend, you should be able to pick up this guide, grab some camp-ing gear and your campmates, and take off to explore. A few of the sites listed may require a short hike to reach the campsite, but most are at or near where you park your car.

This book does not include listings for or information on "commercial" or pri-vately operated campgrounds. While there are some commercial campgrounds in the state, the quality of these facilities is not always constant or consistent. There are directories available listing privately operated facilities, and these directories usual-ly have their own rating systems. RV dealers and suppliers are a good source for such directories. Also, there are no backcountry camping facilities listed in this guide.

With the publicly operated facilities listed here, one can assume at least a basic level of consistency and quality. That being said, even with publicly managed facil-ities, you will find quite a range of quality experiences within these listings. Because Georgia is so diverse in topography, history, and culture, this guide divides the state into four distinct regions, primarily on a geographical basis. They are listed from north to south and include:

- **The Mountains Region,** with some of the more dramatic scenic areas includ-ing the mountains and the northern quarter of the state

- **The Piedmont Region,** the most populous, including metro Atlanta and the foothills south of the mountains

- **The Plains Region,** the geographic and historic heartland, south to the Florida state line

- **The Coastal Region,** including the coastline and areas inland for several miles

Even within these areas you are sure to find enough diversity and difference to keep your interest peaked for quite a few camping adventures. There are many opportunities for fun experiences, from a spur-of-the-moment experimental night at the local state park campground to the well-planned weeklong family camping vacation.

Each region includes individual campsite listings, starting from west to east. Within each listing you will find the following information:

Campground number: Campgrounds within each region are listed in approximate order from west to east. The numbers reflect only the location within the region, not any ranking. You can use the numbers for reference on the locator maps included in each region.

Location: This gives mileage from and location relative to the nearest town or city. This distance is "as the crow flies"; your trip to the campground may include much greater distances on the ground.

Sites: This lists the number and type of sites available in the campground, types of hookups available at those sites, and any restriction on RV or trailer length. Group sites are also indicated here. While many of the campgrounds listed offer group sites, their use is often limited to organized groups such as the Boy or Girl Scouts. Call each campground for specifics on group area usage requirements/restrictions.

Fee per night: Site fees are listed using $$ symbols and are arranged as follows:
$ = less than $10
$$ = $10–$15
$$$ = $16–$20
$$$$ = more than $20
(As site fees change often, this range system is the best way to assure some accuracy within the guide.)

Season: This gives the time of year the campgrounds are open, either spring–fall or year-round. When a campground is listed as being open spring–fall, this generally means April to November, but the months tend to change from year to year depending on the calendar, staffing, etc. Campgrounds in higher elevations have shorter seasons. For specific open times call the campgrounds for more information.

Management: This lists contact information for the agency that manages the campground.

Finding the campground: Directions are given from the nearest town or city name in the "location" heading.

About the campground: This contains information about the campground's setting, special amenities, recreational opportunities in the vicinity, and drawbacks (if any) of camping there.

You will not find any sort of rating system for the campgrounds listed in this guide. Why? First, because the guide only includes campground operated by public agencies; therefore, the quality of is wonderfully consistent across the state. You can visit every campground listed in this guide with the expectation of a safe, secure, and pleasant experience. Second, because different people like different types of campgrounds. There is enough diversity within the state to satisfy almost everyone's preferences on the ideal campground, and to rate campgrounds on my own impression of what's better or worse would only serve to give less credit to some well-run and comfortable campgrounds that just aren't my particular "cup o' tea." For instance, I camp with kids (it's kinda hard to sneak out without them), so I prefer campgrounds with some sort of activities that are reasonably safe for kids and where I can easily watch them from the campsite. In my younger (prekid) days, I preferred to be as far away from "civilization" as possible and would be much more comfortable in an isolated, semideserted backwoods campground with as little reminder of other folks as possible. When we retire, we'll cruise around in an RV, and my preferences will again change, with accessibility and local resources becoming more important. Luckily, no matter what your preferences are, you won't have to leave the state to find what you're looking for.

One other thing to note is that while consistent in quality, the listed campgrounds have a varying degree of handicapped accessibility. When I've listed a campground as being handicapped accessible, this means that, at the minimum, at least one of the rest room facilities at that campground has been modified to accommodate campers with disabilities. Some campgrounds have or are developing handicapped-accessible campsites and recreational facilities as well. For specific information on these facilities, call the campground you are interested in visiting.

With the preceding information in mind, check out this guide, pick a place that looks interesting, and go camping!

The Basics

Georgia is home to an excellent system of roads, from interstate highways to state and county roads. All paved roads are considered year-round. State and county roads in the north part of the state may become more difficult during winter weather, but are generally open all year. Gravel forest roads, most of which are located in the northern half of the state, are more likely to become difficult during inclement weather, and some are closed during the winter. Once out of the mountains, roads should not be too much of a concern when planning your trip. If you have any concerns, contact the agency that manages the campground you're heading for; they can usually supply you with any necessary information. As with any trip, a little planning goes a long way. Take some time before your first trip to list the things you need. Many folks that camp regularly seem to have most of the basic essentials already packed away in containers or in the camper, ready to go at a moment's notice. They just add food and clothes, and they're ready to go. If you're just starting out, here are a few suggestions for basic equipment (some of this may seem pretty obvious, but never underestimate your ability to forget something really important while packing):

- Tent or camper

- Ground cover/barrier for under the tent

- Sleeping bags or bedding for camper

- Air mattress or sleeping pad

- Lantern or light source (more than one source of light is best; lanterns are good for the campsite, and flashlights are good for trips to the privy)

- Extra clothes and socks

- Matches

- Firewood (most campgrounds are pretty well picked clean by early spring)

- Camp stove or cooking rack

- Cooking pans and utensils

- Food

- Water

- Can opener (forgetting this little number can really ruin a weekend if you bring mostly canned foods)

- Toiletries and towels

- Bug repellent and citronella candles

- Basic first-aid supplies

- Ponchos or rain gear

- Trash bags (which also work somewhat when you forget the ponchos)

- Small hand broom or brush

- Plastic or vinyl table cover

- Chairs

- An open mind

And some things to leave behind:

- **Radios or other sources of noise:** Remember that when camping, your "neighbors" are very close and tend to want to spend some time outside as well. Don't screw up someone else's experience by having music blaring at an obnoxious level. And what you consider just right may be too loud to others. (Personally, I think any music other than live by the campfire seems out of place.)

- **Vicious animals.** If your pet is a menace to others, don't bring it to the campground. Period.

- **TVs, video games, computers, and other sorts of modern distractions.** If you want to spend quality time camping, you've got to get rid of all the things that keep you from enjoying the outdoors--basically most things that keep you indoors. Try it: Just say no!

- **Alcohol and drugs.** I'm not talking about a beer or glass of wine here. Some people are so socially inept that they can't "have fun" without the aid of drugs of some sort. If you have to drink or do drugs to have fun, stay at home.

When You Camp with Children

Don't forget that everything might be new to them. While it's almost second nature for you to keep an eye out for snakes or other nasties, children usually aren't paying much attention to such things. And while the basic act of building a fire seems so routine to you, it can be much more meaningful for kids who have never seen such a thing done before. Kids are naturally curious and love to learn new things, especially if they don't think they're learning anything.

Remember too that while kids seem to have an abundance of energy, they are more susceptible to such conditions as dehydration, fatigue, and hypothermia. Keep hikes and outdoor activities to a level manageable for the kids, and always have snacks and water available for them. They'll reward you by always being ready for a new adventure. Pay special attention to younger kids, especially if they haven't had the opportunity to enjoy such places and activities before. Remember, everything's much larger to little ones.

The Boy Scouts and Girl Scouts are excellent groups in which kids can learn many of the basics of camping. These institutions also offer an excellent opportunity for kids and adults to interact in a constructive and instructive atmosphere, and attempt to teach some basic moral and ethical ideals to kids (and adults). If you have or know children of appropriate age, get them (and yourself) involved in these organizations.

Camping with kids can be a lot of hard work on your part to make the experience seem fun to them. But you only have to hear some young voices reaching skyward in a spirited rendition of "Twinkle Twinkle Little Star" at the evening campfire to be reminded what it's really all about.

The Campgrounds

The Mountains Region

Located in the northern part of the state, the Mountains Region offers campers plenty of unique opportunities to experience regional mountain terrain and culture. Isolated backwoods, primitive campgrounds, and nicely appointed lakeside campgrounds with all the amenities are available here. Many of the campgrounds in the Mountains Region are seasonal, usually open from early spring to late fall. Be sure to call the campground you're planning to visit before making the trip. Leaf watchers will enjoy the area in fall, and those wishing to escape from the heat of the lower elevations will find relief here in summer. Spring in the north Georgia mountains is an experience unto itself, and winter can be magical. Just remember to be prepared for changing weather, as conditions in the mountains can change quickly, no matter what the season.

Northwest Georgia Area

1 | Cloudland Canyon State Park

Location: 8 miles east of Trenton.
Sites: 75 tent/trailer/RV sites with water and electricity; maximum RV length 50 feet; 30 walk-in campsites; 4 pioneer campsites; dump station and comfort stations in the improved campground with toilets and showers. Group camping area by reservation only.
Fee per night: $$$$.
Season: Year-round.
Management: Cloudland Canyon State Park, 122 Cloudland Canyon Park Road, Rising Fawn, GA 30738, (706) 657–4050.
Finding the campground: From the intersection of I–59 and Georgia Highway 136, go southeast on GA 136 for 8 miles; the park is on the left.

About the campground: Cloudland, often called Georgia's "Little Grand Canyon," is one of the most scenic parks in the state. The park is centered around a deep gorge cut into the mountain over the eons by Sitton Gulch Creek. Spectacular views abound, and there are hiking trails for the adventurous, both on the rim of the gorge and down to the bottom, where you'll find two scenic waterfalls. Autumn colors are a highlight of this beautiful park. The park encompasses 2,219 acres and includes picnic tables and grills, group picnic shelters, a group lodge, cottages, tennis courts, and a swimming pool. Hiking and mountain biking are available.

2 | James H. "Sloppy" Floyd State Park

Location: 3 miles southeast of Summerville.
Sites: 25 tent/trailer/RV sites, all with water and electricity; maximum RV length 25 feet; dump station and comfort stations with rest rooms and showers. Group camp-

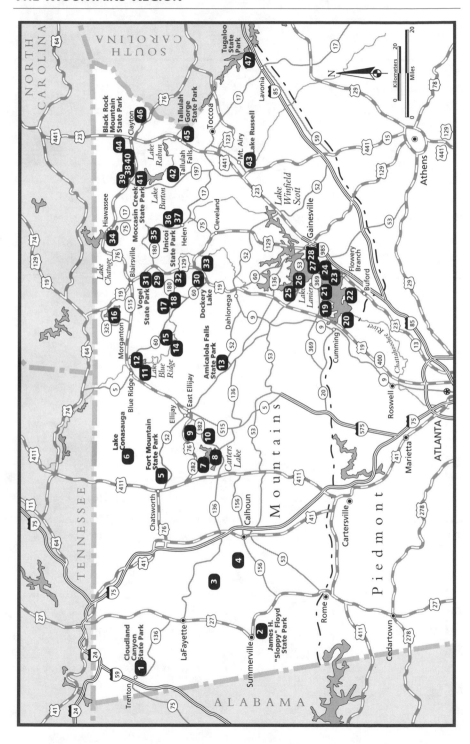

	Group sites	RV	Sites	Max. RV length	Hookups	Toilets	Showers	Coin laundry	Drinking water	Dump	Pets	Handicap Access	Recreation	Fee	Season	Can reserve	Stay limit
1 Cloudland Canyon SP	Y	Y	75	50	WE	F	Y	N	Y	Y	Y	Y	HMST	$$$$		Y	14
2 James H. Sloppy Floyd SP	Y	Y	25	25	WE	F	Y	N	Y	Y	Y	Y	BFHS	$$$$		Y	14
3 Pocket Recreation Area	Y	N	27			F	N	N	Y	N	N	Y	HM	$$	SP–FA	N	14
4 Hidden Creek	N	N	16			F	N	N	Y	N	N	N	FHM		SP–FA	N	14
5 Fort Mountain SP	Y	Y	74	40	WE	F	Y	N	Y	Y	Y	Y	FHMRS	$$$$		Y	14
6 Lake Conasauga	N	Y	35	22		F	Y	N	Y	N	N	Y	FHMOR	$$	SP–FA	N	14
7 Woodring Branch	N	Y	42		WE	F	Y	Y	Y	Y	Y	Y	BFHL	$$$	SP–FA	N	14
8 Doll Mountain	N	Y	58		WE	F	Y			Y	Y	Y	Y	BFHL	$$$	SP–FA	Y	14
9 Harris Branch	Y	N	10			F	Y	Y	Y	N	Y	Y	BFHS	$$	SP–FA	N	14
10 Ridgeway	N	N	22			V	N	N	Y	N	Y	N	BFHLM	$		N	14
11 Lake Blue Ridge	N	Y	54			F	Y	N	Y	N	N	Y	BFHMO	$$	SP–FA	N	14
12 Morganton Point	N	Y	42			F	Y	N	Y	N	N	Y	BFHLS	$$	SP–FA	N	14
13 Amicalola Falls SP	Y	Y	20	17	WE	F	Y	N	Y	Y	Y	Y	HMOR	$$$$		Y	14
14 Frank Gross	N	N	11			F	N	N	Y	N	N	Y	FHM	$$	SP–FA	N	14
15 Deep Hole	N	N	8			V	N	N	Y	N	N	N	FHM	$$		N	14
16 Poteete Creek	N	Y	32	30	WE	F	Y	N	Y	Y	N	Y	BFS	$$		N	14
17 Mulky	N	N	11			F	N	N	Y	N	N	Y	FH	$$	SP–FA	N	14
18 Cooper Creek	N	N	17			F	N	N	Y	N	N	Y	FH	$$	SP–FA	N	14
19 Bald Ridge	N	Y	82	40	WE	F	Y	Y	Y	Y	Y	Y	BFLS	$$$$	SP–FA	Y	14
20 Sawnee	N	Y	56	40	WE	F	Y	Y	Y	Y	Y	Y	BFLS	$$$$	SP–FA	Y	14
21 Shady Grove	Y	Y	113	40	WE	F	Y	Y	Y	Y	Y	Y	BFLS	$$$$	SP–FA	Y	14
22 Shoal Creek	Y	Y	106	40	WE	F	Y	Y	Y	Y	Y	Y	BFLS	$$$$	SP–FA	Y	14
23 Chestnut Ridge	N	Y	85	40	WE	F	Y	Y	Y	Y	Y	Y	BFLS	$$$$	SP–FA	Y	14
24 Old Federal	N	Y	83	40	WE	F	Y	Y	Y	Y	Y	Y	BFLS	$$$$	SP–FA	Y	14
25 Toto Creek	N	Y	9	25		F	N	N	Y	N	Y	N	BFLS	$$	SP–FA	N	14
26 War Hill	N	Y	14	25		F	N	N	Y	N	Y	N	BFLS	$$	SP–FA	N	14
27 Bolding Mill	N	Y	97	40	WE	F	Y	Y	Y	Y	Y	Y	BFLS	$$$$	SP–FA	Y	14
28 Duckett Mill	N	Y	111	40	WE	F	Y	Y	Y	Y	Y	Y	BFLS	$$$$	SP–FA	Y	14
29 Lake Winfield Scott	Y	Y	32	25		F	Y	N	Y	N	N	Y	BFHLS	$$	SP–FA	N	14
30 Dockery Lake	N	Y	10	25		F	N	N	Y	N	N	Y	FH	$$	SP–FA	N	14
31 Vogel SP	Y	Y	95	35	WE	F	Y	N	Y	Y	N	Y	FHS	$$$$		Y	14
32 DeSoto Falls	N	N	24			F	N	N	Y	N	N	Y	FH	$$	SP–FA	N	14
33 Waters Creek	N	N	8			F	N	N	Y	N	N	Y	FH	$$	SP–FA	N	14
34 Lake Chatuge	N	Y	30	25		F	Y	N	Y	N	N	Y	BFHL	$$	SP–FA	N	14
35 Chattahoochee River	N	Y	34	25		F	N	N	Y	N	N	Y	FHM	$$	SP–FA	Y	14

	Group sites	RV	Sites	Max. RV length	Hookups	Toilets	Showers	Coin laundry	Drinking water	Dump	Pets	Handicap Access	Recreation	Fee	Season	Can reserve	Stay limit
36 Andrews Cove	N	Y	10	25		V	N	N	N	N	N	Y	FH	$$	SP–FA	N	14
37 Unicoi SP	Y	Y	52	35	WES	F	Y		Y	Y	Y	Y	FHMS	$$$$		Y	14
38 Tate Branch	N	N	19			F	Y	N	N	N	N	Y	FH	$$		N	14
39 Sandy Bottom	N	N	12			F	N	N	Y	N	N	Y	FH	$$	SP–FA	N	14
40 Tallulah River	N	N	17			V	N	N	Y	N	N	Y	FH	$$	SP–FA	N	14
41 Moccasin Creek SP	Y	Y	54	40	WE	F	Y	Y	Y	Y	Y	Y	BFHL	$$$$		Y	14
42 Rabun Beach	Y	Y	80	40	WE	F	Y	N	Y	Y	N	Y	BFHS	$$$$	SP–FA	Y	14
43 Lake Russell	Y	Y	42	30		F	Y	N	Y	Y	N	Y	BFHL MRS	$$	SP–FA	Y	14
44 Black Rock Mountain SP	Y	Y	59	30	WE	F	Y	Y	Y	Y	Y	Y	FHS	$$$$		Y	14
45 Tallulah Gorge SP	Y	Y	50	40	WE	F	Y	Y	Y	Y	Y	Y	FHLMS	$$		Y	14
46 Willis Knob	N	Y	8	25		F	N	N	Y	N	Y	Y	FHR	$$		Y	14
47 Tugaloo SP	Y	Y	120	35	WE	F	Y	Y	Y	Y	Y	Y	BFHLT	$$$$		Y	14

Hookups: W = Water E = Electric S = Sewer **Toilets:** F = Flush V = Vault **Recreation:** B = Boating F = Fishing G = Golf H = Hiking L = Boat Launch M = Mountain Biking O = Off-Road Vehicles R = Horseback Riding S = Swimming T = Tennis **Fee:** $, less than $10; $$, $10–$15; $$$, $16–$20; $$$$, more than $20. **Maximum RV length** given in feet. **Stay limit** given in days. If no entry under **Season,** campgound is open all year. If no entry under **Fee,** camping is free.

ing area available by reservation only.

Fee per night: $$$$.

Season: Year-round.

Management: James H. "Sloppy" Floyd State Park, Route 1, Box 291, Summerville, GA 30747, (706) 857–0826.

Finding the campground: From Summerville go southeast on U.S. Route 27 for 4 miles. Turn right onto Sloppy Floyd Lake Road to the park entrance.

About the campground: Named after state representative James H. "Sloppy" Floyd, the park features excellent fishing and swimming opportunities on two lakes, a lake boardwalk, and paddleboat rentals. Boats are permitted on the lake (electric motors only). Several picnic areas and a kids' playground make for a nice day by the lake. More adventurous types can enjoy hiking in the adjacent Chattahoochee National Forest.

3 Pocket Recreation Area

Location: About 20 miles southeast of LaFayette.

Sites: 27 tent sites; no utilities; water and flush toilets available on-site. Group camping area available by reservation only.

Fee per night: $$.

Season: Spring–fall.
Management: Chattahoochee/Oconee National Forest, Armuchee District, (706) 638–1085.
Finding the campground: From LaFayette go east on GA 136 for 13.5 miles. Turn right (south) onto Pocket Road and drive 7 miles to the campground.

About the campground: Pocket was the site of a Civilian Conservation Corps camp in the 1930s. The area consists of a large spring and stream surrounded by a wooded glen. Picnic sites and two hiking trails originating from the campground encourage enjoyment of the peaceful locale, and there are some excellent mountain biking trails nearby. The surrounding ridges offer some great views. The camping area offers a group picnic pavilion that will accommodate larger groups.

4 Hidden Creek

Location: About 7 miles west of Calhoun.
Sites: 16 tent sites; no utilities; water and flush toilets on-site.
Fee per night: None.
Season: Spring–fall.
Management: Chattahoochee/Oconee National Forest, Armuchee District, (706) 638–1085.
Finding the campground: From Calhoun go southwest on GA 156 for 7.5 miles. Turn right onto Rock Creek Road and go northwest for 3 miles. Turn right (north) onto Forest Road 955 for 1.3 miles to the campground.

About the campground: Hidden Creek is named after the nearby creek that appears and disappears for days at a time. The campground has picnic areas, but few other facilities, so the only other folks around are anglers, picnickers, other campers, mountain bikers, and hikers enjoying the abundance of local hiking trails. If the quiet surroundings aren't enough, check out the nearby Keown Falls Recreation Area. Otherwise, sit back and enjoy the solitude!

Chatsworth Area

5 Fort Mountain State Park

Location: About 8 miles east of Chatsworth.
Sites: 74 tent/RV sites with water and electricity, including 35 pull-throughs; maximum RV length 40 feet; 3 primitive backcountry sites; pioneer group campsite; dump station and comfort stations with toilets and showers. Group camping area available by reservation only.
Fee per night: $$$$.
Season: Year-round.
Management: Fort Mountain State Park, (706) 695–2621. Reservations: (800) 864–7275.

Finding the campground: From Chatsworth go east on GA 52 for 8 miles; the park is on the left.

About the campground: One of my personal favorites, Fort Mountain State Park has some of everything for the camping adventurer: a lake with swimming beach; paddleboat rentals; a pathway around the shore; plenty of picnic tables and shelters; miniature golf; and the interesting ruins of an 855-foot-long rock wall, the "fort" for which the mountain is named and the origins of which are still in doubt. For even more fun and some great exercise, the park has 14 miles of hiking trails and has recently added more than 25 miles of mountain bike trails and another 20 miles of horse trails. Horse rentals are available at the stables on the lower slopes of the mountain. If you're into fishing, hiking, mountain biking, or horseback riding, Fort Mountain makes a great destination.

6 Lake Conasauga

Location: About 9.5 miles northeast of Chatsworth.
Sites: 35 sites; no utilities; 22-foot-maximum RV/trailer length; comfort station with flush toilets, showers, and water on-site.
Fee per night: $$.
Season: Spring–fall.
Management: Chattahoochee/Oconee National Forest, Cohutta District, (706) 695–6736.
Finding the campground: From Chatsworth go north on U.S. Route 411 for 4 miles. Turn right at the traffic light in Eton and follow FR 18 (CCC Camp Road) east for 10 miles. Turn left onto FR 68 and go northeast 10 miles to the campground (you will go through two intersections on the way; follow the signs).

About the campground: Nineteen-acre Lake Conasauga is the highest lake in Georgia. The drive to the campground on gravel forest roads that climb almost 2,000 feet can be somewhat of a challenge; the road is steep and curvy and contains sections of "washboard" that will get your attention if you go too fast. Upon arriving at the campground, you'll be rewarded with a most scenic area, and the options of fishing, horseback riding, hiking, and picnicking are enough to keep almost everyone entertained. There are mountain bike and off-road-vehicle trails nearby for those who want more options. Take some time to enjoy viewing the abundant wildlife in the area and the quiet beauty of the surrounding forest. It's no wonder Lake Conasauga lures campers back again year after year.

Carters Lake Area

7 Woodring Branch

Location: About 11 miles southeast of Chatsworth.
Sites: 31 tent/camper/RV sites with water and electricity; 11 tent sites, no utilities;

dump station and comfort stations with toilets, showers, and coin laundry on-site.
Fee per night: $$$.
Season: Spring–fall.
Management: U.S. Army Corps of Engineers, (877) 444–6777.
Finding the campground: From Chatsworth go south on U.S. Route 441 for just more than 5 miles. Turn left onto U.S. Route 76/GA 282 and follow it for 5 miles. Look for the entrance road on the right.

About the campground: Carters Lake is a popular favorite; the boat ramp and dock make things easy for boaters and anglers. The deep lake and surrounding hilly topography make for some great scenery any time of year. There's a playground on-site for the littler folk and hiking trails for everyone to enjoy. The campground also has an amphitheater for seasonal presentations.

8 Doll Mountain

Location: About 10 miles southwest of East Ellijay.
Sites: 39 tent/RV sites with water and electricity; 19 tent sites; dump station and comfort stations with toilets and showers on-site.
Fee per night: $$$.
Season: Spring–fall.
Management: U.S. Army Corps of Engineers, (877) 444–6777.
Finding the campground: From the intersection of GA 515 and U.S. Route 76 in East Ellijay, go south on GA 515 for 5 miles. Turn right onto GA 382. Follow GA 382 for 10 miles. The entrance to Doll Mountain is on the right.

About the campground: Doll Mountain offers another opportunity to enjoy scenic Carters Lake. The area includes a boat ramp and dock, a playground, and an amphitheater. The lake, where one can fish, is the primary focus of the campground, and a hiking trail offers additional opportunity to enjoy the surroundings.

9 Harris Branch

Location: About 10 miles southwest of East Ellijay.
Sites: 10 tent sites; no utilities; comfort stations with toilets, showers, water, and coin laundry on-site. Group camping area available by reservation only.
Fee per night: $$.
Season: Spring–fall.
Management: U.S. Army Corps of Engineers, (877) 444–6777.
Finding the campground: From Ellijay go south on Old GA 5. Turn right on GA 382 and go 8.9 miles to the park entrance on the right. Turn right and go 1.5 miles to the campground.

About the campground: Harris Branch, while offering only primitive campsites, still enjoys the luxury of comfort stations and the accompanying ease of camping that such facilities bring. There is also a playground for the little ones, hiking, fishing, boating, and a public beach so everyone can enjoy the cool blue waters of Carters Lake.

10 Ridgeway

Location: About 10 miles west of East Ellijay.
Sites: 22 tent sites; no utilities; drinking water and vault toilets on-site.
Fee per night: $.
Season: Year-round.
Management: U.S. Army Corps of Engineers, (877) 444–6777.
Finding the campground: From the intersection of GA 515 and U.S. Route 76 in East Ellijay, go west on U.S. Route 76 for 8.5 miles. Turn left by Paw-Paw's store, and go 3.1 miles to the campground.

About the campground: Unlike the other three Corps of Engineers campgrounds on Carters Lake, Ridgeway is open year-round. There are no facilities other than vault toilets, and a boat ramp and parking lot accommodate boaters. The Ridgeway Bike Trail, which leaves from and returns to the parking lot, provides a challenging workout, as well as some nice scenery for mountain bikers. The area also has a short hiking trail. Visitors to Ridgeway will enjoy the quiet scenery of the lake—a good place to fish—and the surrounding woods, and the solitude that results from the campground's location.

Blue Ridge Area

11 Lake Blue Ridge

Location: About 2.5 miles southeast of Blue Ridge.
Sites: 48 tent/RV sites; 6 tent sites, no utilities; comfort stations with flush toilets, showers, and water on-site.
Fee per night: $$.
Season: Spring–fall.
Management: Chattahoochee/Oconee National Forest, Toccoa District, East Main Street, Box 1839, Blue Ridge, GA 30513, (706) 632–3031.
Finding the campground: From Blue Ridge go east on East First Street (old U.S. Route 76) for 1.5 miles to Dry Branch Road. Turn right (south), and travel 3 miles to the campground entrance.

About the campground: Lake Blue Ridge is a beautiful place to spend a weekend or a year. The surrounding peaks offer striking contrast to the blue waters of the lake. Like most national forest campgrounds, this one has fewer man-made improvements but offers more in the way of peace and quiet amid a natural setting. The lake offers plenty of boating and fishing activities, and there is a short hiking trail at the campground. The nearby Aska Trails Area contains some of the area's best hiking, mountain biking, and off-road-vehicle trails.

⏷ Morganton Point (Lake Blue Ridge)

Location: 1 mile southwest of Morganton.
Sites: 28 tent/RV sites; 14 tent sites, no utilities; comfort stations with flush toilets, showers, and water on-site.
Fee per night: $$.
Season: Spring–fall.
Management: Chattahoochee/Oconee National Forest, Toccoa District, (706) 632–3031.
Finding the campground: From Morganton go west on Country Road 616 for 1 mile to the campground entrance.

About the campground: Situated on the northeast end of Lake Blue Ridge, Morganton Point is one of two Forest Service campgrounds on the lake. The area has plenty of lake and mountain views, as well as lake access via a boat ramp. Several of the campsites overlook the lake, and most of the campground is wooded enough to feel private. Boating, swimming, skiing, and fishing are favorite pursuits on the scenic lake, as is just relaxing and hiking around the surroundings.

⏷ Amicalola Falls State Park

Location: 16 miles west of Dahlonega.
Sites: 20 tent/RV sites with water and electricity, including 3 pull-throughs; maximum RV length 17 feet; dump station and comfort stations with flush toilets, showers, and water on-site. Group camping area available by reservation only.
Fee per night: $$$$.
Season: Year-round.
Management: Amicalola Falls State Park and Lodge, (800) 573–9656.
Finding the campground: From Dahlonega go west on GA 9 for 3.5 miles. Turn right (west) onto GA 52 and go 15 miles. The park entrance is on the right.

About the campground: Amicalola Falls, from which the park gets its name, is at 729 feet the highest waterfall in Georgia. The park is divided into two areas: The visitor center/museum and cottages are at the base of the falls; the campground, more cottages, a lodge, and a hike-in campground are near the top of the falls. The road to the top of the falls and the campground, while paved, is steep in sections, but the views, surroundings, and campground are well worth the trip. The park provides access to the Appalachian Trail via an 8-mile approach trail that leads to Springer Mountain, the southern terminus of the AT. There are other hiking trails in the park, and the campground is the starting point for a longtime favorite mountain bike loop. More adventurous (or fit) campers can hike the 5.5 miles to the new Leonard E. Foote Walk-In Lodge and can ride horses and off-road vehicles.

14 Frank Gross

Location: About 15 miles south of Morganton.
Sites: 11 tent sites; no utilities; drinking water and flush toilets available on-site.

Fee per night: $$.
Season: Spring–fall.
Management: Chattahoochee-Oconee National Forest, Toccoa District, (706) 632–3031.
Finding the campground: From Morganton go south on GA 60 for 15 miles. Turn right (south) onto Forest Road 69, and travel 5 miles to the campground.

About the campground: Frank Gross sits on the banks of Rock Creek, and it's pretty obvious how this creek got its name. The water tumbles and splashes noisily over rocks and boulders, and through mountain vegetation, giving one a wonderful sense of isolation and serenity. The trout fishing is some of the best around, and a visit to the nearby Chattahoochee National Forest Fish Hatchery is good fun for the sportsperson and fish-junky. For those who don't fish, there is also hiking and mountain biking. The surroundings at this campground make it worth the extended trip to get here.

15 Deep Hole

Location: About 13 miles southeast of Morganton.
Sites: 8 tent sites; no utilities; vault toilets and drinking water available on-site.
Fee per night: $$.
Season: Year-round.
Management: Chattahoochee/Oconee National Forest, Toccoa District, (706) 632–3031.
Finding the campground: From Morganton go south on GA 60 for 16 miles to the campground.

About the campground: Deep Hole is right on the Toccoa River, and the surrounding mountains and dense forest make for a real backwoods feel. The fishing is pretty good along the river, and there are hiking trails in the area as well. One of the smallest national forest campgrounds, the scenery surrounding Deep Hole is perfect for those who want to feel like they're "getting away from it all." For anglers, the nearby Chattahoochee National Forest Fish Hatchery is an interesting diversion. A canoe launch at the campsite offers more waterborne activities. The abundance of forest roads in the area also provides lots of opportunity for walking and mountain biking.

16 Poteete Creek

Location: About 8.5 miles northwest of Blairsville.
Sites: 25 tent/RV sites with water and electricity; 7 tent sites, no utilities; maximum RV length 30 feet; dump station and comfort station with flush toilets and showers on-site.
Fee per night: $$.
Season: Year-round.
Management: Tennessee Valley Authority (TVA), (706) 745–5614.
Finding the campground: From Blairsville go northwest on U.S. Route 19/129 for

9.3 miles. Turn left (west) onto GA 325 and go 3.5 miles. Turn left (east) at the directional sign, and travel 1 mile to the campground.

About the campground: One of TVA's only campgrounds in Georgia, Poteete Creek is located on the shores of beautiful Nottely Lake. The surrounding terrain and scenery make the campground a pleasant destination, and the sites are well situated on the shores of the lake. Facilities/activities include a swimming area, picnic area, and fishing. The area around Blairsville is some of north Georgia's most scenic, and the town itself makes an interesting day trip.

17   Mulky

Location: About 12 miles southeast of Morganton.
Sites: 11 tent sites; no utilities; flush toilets and drinking water on-site.
Fee per night: $$.
Season: Spring–fall.
Management: Chattahoochee/Oconee National Forest, Toccoa District, (706) 632–3031.
Finding the campground: From Morganton go south on GA 60 for 15.8 miles. Turn left (east) onto Cooper Creek Road (Forest Road 4) and go 5 miles to the campground.

About the campground: Mulky lies along Cooper Creek, which is known locally for some pretty good trout fishing. If you enjoy trout fishing, you'll enjoy Mulky. Like most national forest campgrounds, it feels more isolated than it is, and the surroundings make for a pretty good wilderness experience. The abundant wildlife and beautiful plants in the area provide some good nature-watching to complement the fishing. Hikers can enjoy nearby Yellow Mountain Trail and other excellent trails in the area.

18   Cooper Creek

Location: About 12.5 miles southeast of Morganton.
Sites: 17 tent sites; no utilities; flush toilets and drinking water on-site.
Fee per night: $$.
Season: Spring–fall.
Management: Chattahoochee/Oconee National Forest, Toccoa District, (706) 632–3031.
Finding the campground: From Morganton go south on GA 60 for 15.8 miles. Turn left (east) onto Cooper Creek Road (Forest Road 4), and go 6 miles. Turn right onto FR 236; the campground is on the left.

About the campground: Like nearby Mulky, this campground is set next to Cooper Creek. The creek is stocked with trout and is a favorite for anglers. Four of the campsites are located right next to the creek. The campground's location and setting gives one a feeling of being in the wilderness. Hikers can enjoy three relatively short trails nearby that offer plenty of opportunity for experiencing the beauty of the surrounding terrain and wildlife.

Lake Lanier Area

19 Bald Ridge

Location: About 3 miles east of Cumming.
Sites: 82 tent/RV sites with water and electricity, including 15 pull-throughs; maximum RV length 40 feet; dump station and comfort stations with toilets, showers, and coin laundry on-site.
Fee per night: $$$$.
Season: Spring–fall.
Management: U.S. Army Corps of Engineers, P.O. Box 657, Buford, GA 31515, (770) 945–9531.
Finding the campground: From exit 16 off GA 400, go southeast on Pilgrim Mill Road for 0.3 mile. Bear right (south) on Sinclair Shoals Road for 1.9 miles. Turn left on Bald Ridge Road and follow it to the campground.

About the campground: Bald Ridge is one of eleven Corps of Engineers campgrounds around Lake Sidney Lanier. The lake is one of the busiest in the country, with fishing, skiing, sailing, and all sorts of other things going on just about anytime during the season. The campground features picnic tables, a boat ramp, and a swimming area on-site, so campers can spend as much time on or in the water as they wish. Some of the sites are right on the water.

20 Sawnee

Location: About 4.5 miles southeast of Cumming.
Sites: 56 tent/RV sites with water and electricity, including 6 pull-throughs; maximum RV length 40 feet; dump station and comfort stations with toilets, showers, and coin laundry on-site.
Fee per night: $$$$.
Season: Spring–fall.
Management: U.S. Army Corps of Engineers, P.O. Box 657, Buford, GA 31515, (770) 945–9531.
Finding the campground: From the intersection of U.S. Route 19/GA 9 and Buford Dam Road, go east on Buford Dam Road for 4 miles. The campground is on your left.

About the campground: Lake Lanier is also the focus of this campground. Situated on the southeastern end of the lake, Sawnee's facilities include a boat ramp, swimming area, and picnic tables, and there's fishing on the lake. Water lovers will appreciate the convenient location of the campground to other lake facilities. Those not so water-oriented and the kiddies will enjoy the campground's playground and surroundings.

21 Shady Grove

Location: About 6.5 miles east of Cumming.

Sites: 76 tent/RV sites with water and electricity; 37 tent sites, no utilities; maximum RV length 40 feet; dump station and comfort stations with flush toilets, showers, and coin laundry on-site. Group camping area available by reservation only.

Fee per night: $$$$.

Season: Spring–fall.

Management: U.S. Army Corps of Engineers, P.O. Box 657, Buford, GA 31515, (770) 945–9531.

Finding the campground: From Cumming go north on GA 400 to exit 17, GA 306. Turn right (east) onto GA 306, and go 1 mile to GA 369. Turn right (east) onto GA 369 and go 2 miles to Shady Grove Road. Turn right onto Shady Grove Road, which ends at the campground.

About the campground: Shady Grove is located on the north side of the lake on the southeast end. The campground sits on a small peninsula with water on three sides, which is great for fishing. The campground features a boat ramp, swimming area, picnic tables, and a playground. This campground has an abundance of sites without utilities, which tent campers seem to prefer. Many of the sites are on or overlooking the lake.

22 Shoal Creek

Location: About 3 miles north of Buford.

Sites: 47 tent/RV sites with water and electricity, including 14 pull-throughs; maximum RV length 40 feet; 59 tent sites, no utilities; dump station and comfort stations with flush toilets, showers, and coin laundry on-site. Group camping area available by reservation only.

Fee per night: $$$$.

Season: Spring–fall.

Management: U.S. Army Corps of Engineers, P.O. Box 657, Buford, GA 31515, (770) 945–9531.

Finding the campground: From Buford go north on Peachtree Industrial Boulevard for 2 miles. Turn left (north) onto Shadburn Ferry Road. Go 2.8 miles; the road dead-ends at the campground.

About the campground: Shoal Creek is the southernmost campground on Lake Lanier. The campground lies on a peninsula and is surrounded by water on three sides, giving many of the sites access to the water and great views of the lake. A boat ramp, swimming area, picnic tables, playground, and fishing provide ample opportunities for entertainment. The campground is convenient to Buford should campers feel the need for civilization's perks.

ⓔ Chestnut Ridge

Location: About 2.5 miles west of Flowery Branch.
Sites: 51 tent/RV sites with water and electricity, including 4 pull-throughs; maximum RV length 40 feet; 34 tent sites, no utilities; dump stations and comfort stations with flush toilets, showers, and coin laundry on-site.
Fee per night: $$$$.
Season: Spring–fall.
Management: U.S. Army Corps of Engineers, P.O. Box 657, Buford, GA 31515, (770) 945–9531.
Finding the campground: From Flowery Branch go south on GA 13 for 1.8 miles. Turn right (west) onto Gaines Ferry Road, and go 3 miles. Turn right (north) onto Chestnut Ridge Road. The road ends at the campground.

About the campground: Another lake lover's camping paradise, Chestnut Ridge has all the things for water lovers and their families: boat ramp, swimming area, fishing area, picnic tables, and a playground. Many of the sites are on the lakeshore or overlook the water; the interior sites offer a little more privacy.

ⓐ Old Federal

Location: About 3 miles north of Flowery Branch.
Sites: 59 tent/RV sites with water and electricity, including 10 pull-throughs; maximum RV length 40 feet; 24 tent sites, no utilities; dump stations and comfort stations with flush toilets, showers, and coin laundry on-site.
Fee per night: $$$$.
Season: Spring–fall.
Management: U.S. Army Corps of Engineers, P.O. Box 657, Buford, GA 31515, (770) 945–9531.
Finding the campground: From Flowery Branch go north on McEver Road to Jim Crow Road. Turn left (north) onto Jim Crow Road, and travel 3 miles to the campground.

About the campground: The Corps of Engineers does a great job locating their campgrounds on peninsulas so that there's water on three sides. Old Federal is a good example of this practice. The campground's shoreline provides opportunities for fishing, boating, swimming, and other water sports. The area also includes picnic tables, a playground, and a boat launch. Many sites overlook the lake, and the interior sites are nicely wooded and more private.

25 Toto Creek

Location: About 14 miles northeast of Cumming.
Sites: 9 tent/RV sites; maximum RV length 25 feet; no utilities; drinking water and flush toilets on-site.

Fee per night: $$.

Season: Spring–fall.

Management: U.S. Army Corps of Engineers, P.O. Box 657, Buford, GA 31515, (770) 945–9531.

Finding the campground: From Cumming go north on GA 400 for 17 miles. Turn right onto GA 136, and travel 2 miles to the campground.

About the campground: Toto Creek is located on the northern, less developed part of Lake Lanier. The sites have no utilities but are nicely spaced and located. A boat ramp and picnic tables are on-site, as well as a swimming area. There's also fishing. If you want to spend time on the lake but prefer less crowded conditions (relatively speaking), then Toto Creek is a good bet.

26 War Hill

Location: About 15 miles northeast of Cumming.

Sites: 14 tent/RV sites; maximum RV length 25 feet; no utilities; drinking water and flush toilets on-site.

Fee per night: $$.

Season: Spring–fall.

Management: U.S. Army Corps of Engineers, P.O. Box 657, Buford, GA 31515, (770) 945–9531.

Finding the campground: From Cumming go north on GA 400 to GA 53. Turn right (southeast) onto GA 53 and go 4 miles. Turn left (east) onto War Hill Park Road, and follow it to the campground.

About the campground: War Hill is located on the slightly less developed north end of Lake Lanier. The sites are well located on a peninsula, surrounded on three sides by water. Though the sites have no utilities, the campground is very pleasant, and most sites offer views of or are next to the water. The prerequisite boat ramp and swimming area on-site cater to the lake lovers and anglers. One of the smaller campgrounds on the lake, War Hill offers a somewhat quieter way to enjoy the lake atmosphere.

27 Bolding Mill

Location: About 7 miles west of Gainesville.

Sites: 88 tent/RV sites with water and electricity, including 5 pull-throughs; maximum RV length 40 feet; 9 tent sites, no utilities; dump stations and comfort stations with flush toilets, showers, and coin laundry on-site.

Fee per night: $$$$.

Season: Spring–fall.

Management: U.S. Army Corps of Engineers, P.O. Box 657, Buford, GA 31515, (770) 945–9531.

Finding the campground: From Gainesville go west on GA 53 for 4.9 miles to Sardis Road. Turn right (north) and go 0.5 mile. Turn left onto Chestatee Road, and follow it to the campground.

About the campground: Bolding Mill, though just across a narrow part of the lake from War Hill Park, is a much larger campground, with several arms jutting out into the water. Although the campground is larger, most of the sites are still well situated, nicely spaced, and conveniently located to comfort stations and other facilities. A boat ramp, swimming area, picnic tables, a playground, and fishing ensure lots of entertainment for everyone.

28 | Duckett Mill

Location: About 6 miles west of Gainesville.
Sites: 97 tent/RV sites with water and electricity, including 9 pull-throughs; maximum RV length 40 feet; 14 tent sites, no utilities; dump station and comfort stations with flush toilets, showers, and coin laundry on-site.
Fee per night: $$$$.
Season: Spring–fall.
Management: U.S. Army Corps of Engineers, P.O. Box 657, Buford, GA 31515, (770) 945–9531.
Finding the campground: From Gainesville go west on GA 53 for 5.1 miles. Turn left (south) onto Duckett Mill Road, which ends at the campground.

About the campground: Duckett Mill is closest to Gainesville and offers full amenities for campers. The campground is spread over several arms of land reaching into the lake, which gives many of the sites direct access to the lake. A boat ramp is on-site, as well as a swimming area, picnic area, and a playground. There's also fishing on the lake. The interior sites are reasonably private, offering more trees as a trade-off for not being on the water. A short stroll from anywhere in the campground offers easy access to the lake.

Blairsville and Hiawassee Area

29 | Lake Winfield Scott

Location: About 10 miles south of Blairsville.
Sites: 21 tent/RV sites, including 6 pull-throughs; maximum RV length 25 feet; 11 tent sites, no utilities; comfort stations with water, flush toilets, and showers on-site. Group camping area available by reservation only.
Fee per night: $$.
Season: Spring–fall.
Management: Chattahoochee-Oconee National Forest, Brasstown District, (706) 745–6928.
Finding the campground: From Blairsville go south on U.S. Route 19/129 for 10 miles. Turn right (west) onto GA 180 and travel 6.9 miles to the campground.

About the campground: Eighteen-acre Lake Winfield Scott is a local favorite for fishing. The lake is stocked with rainbow trout, as well as other local species. There is a footpath around the lake, part of which is paved and wheelchair accessible, as is the dock. Facilities include a boat ramp (electric motors only), a sand swimming area, and a playground. The scenery around the lake and two hiking trails offer other opportunities for postfishing entertainment. There are two double sites available for families and a group camping area, available by reservation only.

0 Dockery Lake

Location: About 10 miles north of Dahlonega.
Sites: 5 tent/RV sites; maximum RV length 25 feet; 5 tent sites, no utilities; drinking water and flush toilets are available on-site.
Fee per night: $$.
Season: Spring–fall.
Management: Chattahoochee-Oconee National Forest, Brasstown District, (706) 745–6928.
Finding the campground: From Dahlonega go north on GA 60 for 11 miles. Turn right (northeast) onto Forest Road 654, and travel 1 mile to the campground.

About the campground: Dockery Lake is a three-acre mountain lake stocked with rainbow trout and other native species of fish, making it especially popular with anglers. The campground is in a wooded area overlooking the lake, and some of the sites are on the shore. The surrounding woods give a good impression of being isolated. There are two hiking trails in the area, one of which connects with the Appalachian Trail. If you like fishing in scenic surroundings, you'll enjoy Dockery Lake.

1 Vogel State Park

Location: About 11 miles south of Blairsville.
Sites: 95 tent/RV sites with water and electricity, including 18 pull-throughs; maximum RV length 35 feet; dump station and comfort stations with flush toilets and showers on-site. Group camping area available by reservation only.
Fee per night: $$$$.
Season: Year-round.
Management: Vogel State Park, (706) 745–2628. Reservations: (800) 864–7275.
Finding the campground: From Blairsville go south on U.S. Route 19/129 for 11 miles. The park is on the right.

About the campground: Vogel is one of Georgia's oldest and most popular state parks, the work of the Civilian Conservation Corps. There is a small museum on-site dedicated to the CCC. The park features a small lake with paddleboat rentals, a swimming area, and a special fishing area just for kids. Miniature golf, picnic areas, and a hiking trail offer lots to do for families with kids. The surrounding area offers much in the way of rugged mountain scenery, and the fall colors are especially beautiful. The sites are a little closer together than in some larger parks, but for families and folks looking for activities, Vogel is a great destination.

32 DeSoto Falls

Location: About 15 miles northwest of Cleveland.
Sites: 24 tent sites, no utilities; comfort stations with flush toilets and water on-site.
Fee per night: $$.
Season: Spring–fall.
Management: Chattahoochee-Oconee National Forest, Brasstown District, (706) 745–6928.
Finding the campground: From Cleveland go north on U.S. Route 129 for 15 miles. The campground is on the left.

About the campground: This campground is located within the DeSoto Falls Scenic Area, a rugged, picturesque area featuring several beautiful waterfalls. The campground lies along the wooded banks of Frogtown Creek, where one can fish, and several of the sites are close to the creek. The music of tumbling waters provides a perfect lullaby to snooze by. The nearby DeSoto Falls hiking trail is a must for waterfall watchers, and the flora and fauna of the surrounding mountain ecology provide a wonderful backdrop for a real mountain camping experience.

33 Waters Creek

Location: About 10 miles north of Dahlonega.
Sites: 8 tent sites; no utilities; drinking water and flush toilets on-site.
Fee per night: $$.
Season: Spring–fall.
Management: Chattahoochee-Oconee National Forest, Brasstown District, (706) 745–6928.
Finding the campground: From Dahlonega go north on U.S. Route 19 north for 12 miles. Turn left (northwest) onto Forest Road 34, and travel 1 mile to the campground.

About the campground: Waters Creek sits on a picturesque mountain stream that tumbles over rocks and through mountain laurel and rhododendron. The sites are located on the banks of the creek—which has good fishing—and offer an opportunity to sample the peace and solitude of the mountain surroundings, by hiking or simply relaxing. The campground is small enough to feel uncrowded, even when completely full. If you prefer nature for your surroundings, you'll enjoy Waters Creek.

34 Lake Chatuge

Location: About 2 miles west of Hiawassee.
Sites: 20 tent/RV sites; maximum RV length 25 feet; 10 tent sites, no utilities; comfort stations with drinking water, showers, and flush toilets on-site.
Fee per night: $$.
Season: Spring–fall.
Management: Chattahoochee-Oconee National Forest, Brasstown District, (706) 745–6928.

Finding the campground: From Hiawassee go northwest on U.S. Route 76 for 1.8 miles. Turn left (south) onto GA 288, and travel 1 mile to the campground.

About the campground: The campground is located on a peninsula that reaches out into the 7,000-acre Tennessee Valley Authority Lake Chatuge. Most of the campsites enjoy a nice view of the lake. Facilities include a boat ramp and picnic tables. There are some nice fishing spots along the lake, and a 1.3-mile footpath skirts the campground along the shore. Nearby Hiawassee makes for a fun day trip when you're tired of fishing (as if!).

Helen Area

35 Chattahoochee River

Location: About 10 miles north of Helen.
Sites: 24 tent/RV sites; maximum RV length 25 feet; 10 tent sites, no utilities; drinking water and flush toilets on-site.
Fee per night: $$.
Season: Spring–fall.
Management: Chattahoochee-Oconee National Forest, Chattooga District, (706) 754–6221.
Finding the campground: From Helen go north on GA 75 for 1 mile. Turn left (west) onto GA 75 Alternate, and cross the river. Just after crossing the river, turn right onto Forest Road 44. Follow FR 44 for 9.2 miles; the campground is on the left.

About the campground: Chattahoochee River is a treat; even the drive up the curvy, narrow, gravel forest road is beautiful. The campground is nestled among the tumbling headwaters of the Chattahoochee River, and the surrounding mountain hardwood forest is a sensory treat. Several sites overlook the river, where there's fishing, and others are somewhat hidden back in the surrounding trees. Hikers can enjoy nearby Horse Trough Falls, or the Mark Trail Wilderness Area, just back down FR 44. There are several good mountain bike rides in the area, including one that follows FR 44 past the campground. Visit nearby Helen for some interesting shops and some pretty good restaurants.

36 Andrews Cove

Location: About 6 miles north of Helen.
Sites: 5 tent/RV sites; maximum RV length 25 feet; 5 tent sites, no utilities; vault toilets on-site.
Fee per night: $$.
Season: Spring–fall.
Management: Chattahoochee-Oconee National Forest, Chattooga District, (706) 754–6221.

Finding the campground: From Helen go north on GA 17/75 for 6 miles. The campground is on the right.

About the campground: Andrews Creek is a typical tumbling, noisy, beautiful mountain stream surrounded by mature trees and natural undergrowth. The campsites sit along the banks of the creek. Trout fishing is an attractive option for sportspersons, though the surroundings make catching fish almost an interruption. Hikers can enjoy the 2-mile Andrews Cove Trail, which connects to the nearby Appalachian Trail. Take some time and visit nearby Helen, a faux Bavarian village tourist destination with some surprisingly good restaurants and shops. The entire area around the campground contains some of Georgia's most scenic mountain terrain.

37 | Unicoi State Park

Location: 2 miles northeast of Helen.
Sites: 40 tent/RV sites with water and electricity; maximum RV length 35 feet; 12 tent/RV sites with water, sewer, and electricity; dump station and comfort stations with flush toilets and showers on-site. Group camping area available by reservation only.
Fee per night: $$$$.
Season: Year-round.
Management: Unicoi State Park, (706) 878–3982. Reservations: (800) 864–7275.
Finding the campground: From Helen go northwest on GA 75 for 1 mile. Turn right (north) onto GA 356, and travel 1.3 miles; the lodge is to your right and the campground is to your left.

About the campground: The campground at Unicoi sits on the shores of fifty-three-acre Unicoi Lake. Some of the campsites are near the lake, but most are back in the trees, some along a mountain stream. Facilities include a swimming area, a dock for fishing, canoe and paddleboat rentals, hiking trails, and a mountain bike trail. You can mountain bike or hike via a connector trail to nearby Helen and enjoy the shops and restaurants there. The Unicoi Lodge and Conference Center, just across GA 356 but still within the park, also has a good buffet-style restaurant. Whether you enjoy few conveniences or many, Unicoi can deliver.

Clayton and Tallulah Gorge Area

38 | Tate Branch

Location: About 13 miles northwest of Clayton.
Sites: 15 tent/RV sites; 4 tent sites, no utilities; comfort stations with flush toilets and showers on-site.
Fee per night: $$.
Season: Year-round.

Management: Chattahoochee-Oconee National Forest, Tallulah District, (706) 782–3320.

Finding the campground: From Clayton go west on U.S. Route 76 for 8 miles. Turn right (north) onto an unnumbered paved county road, and go 4 miles. Turn left (northwest) onto Forest Road 70, and travel 4 miles to the campground.

About the campground: FR 70 is somewhat steep and winding in places, and the drive to the campground can be an adventure. This somewhat remote campground is located at the junction of the Tallulah River and Tate Branch. The drive is well worth it; the campground feels very isolated and well away from things, though the sites are a little closer together than in some other national forest campgrounds in the area. Hiking is available in the nearby Coleman River Scenic Area, and anglers will enjoy the trout fishing in both the river and the creek.

39 Sandy Bottom

Location: About 15 miles northwest of Clayton.
Sites: 12 tent sites, no utilities; flush toilets and water on-site.
Fee per night: $$.
Season: Spring–fall.
Management: Chattahoochee-Oconee National Forest, Tallulah District, (706) 782–3320.
Finding the campground: From Clayton go west on U.S. Route 76 for 8 miles. Turn right (north) onto an unnumbered paved county road and go 4 miles. Turn left (northwest) onto Forest Road 70, and go 5 miles to the campground.

About the campground: Sandy Bottom is a lot like Tate Branch. The campground sits along the Tallulah River, which splashes pleasantly through the wilderness. The remoteness of the campground and the surrounding scenery make this one well worth the drive. Trout fishing is a favorite local pastime, and hikers will enjoy the nearby Coleman River Trail. For the seeker of beauty, solitude, and a feeling of isolation, Sandy Bottom offers the perfect answer.

40 Tallulah River

Location: About 9 miles west of Clayton.
Sites: 17 tent sites, no utilities; drinking water and vault toilets on-site.
Fee per night: $$.
Season: Spring–fall.
Management: Chattahoochee-Oconee National Forest, Tallulah District, (706) 782–3320.
Finding the campground: From Clayton go west on U.S. Route 76 for 8 miles. Turn right (north) onto an unnumbered paved county road, and travel 4 miles. Turn left (northwest) onto Forest Road 70, and travel 1 mile to the campground.

About the campground: Located next to the beautiful Tallulah River, the campground, like Sandy Bottom and Tate Branch, will place you in the middle of some beautiful scenery. Like the other two campgrounds, the trout fishing here is good.

Hiking is available nearby, and the towns of Tallulah Falls and Hiawassee make for interesting day trips. Though remote, this campground is well worth the trip.

41 Moccasin Creek State Park

Location: About 18 miles west of Clayton.
Sites: 54 tent/RV sites with water and electricity; maximum RV length 40 feet; dump station and comfort stations with flush toilets, showers, and coin laundry on-site. Group camping area available by reservation only.
Fee per night: $$$$.
Season: Year-round.
Management: Moccasin Creek State Park, (706) 947–3194. Reservations: (800) 864–7275.
Finding the campground: From Clayton go west on U.S. Route 76 for 12 miles. Turn left (south) onto GA 197 to the campground.

About the campground: Located on Lake Burton, Moccasin Creek, though small, is packed with things to see and do. The park offers an interpretive trail for nature enthusiasts and a 2-mile hiking trail. There is a boat ramp and dock, and a wheelchair-accessible fishing pier for the mobility-challenged. A playground offers entertainment for young campers, and the nearby towns of Clayton and Clarkesville offer good options for day trips.

42 Rabun Beach

Location: About 11 miles south of Clayton.
Sites: 80 tent/RV sites with water and electricity; maximum RV length 40 feet; dump station and comfort station with flush toilets and showers on-site. Group camping area available by reservation only.
Fee per night: $$$$.
Season: Spring–fall.
Management: Chattahoochee-Oconee National Forest, Tallulah District, (706) 782–3320.
Finding the campground: From Clayton go south on U.S. Route 441/23 for 6.9 miles. Turn right (west) onto an unnumbered county road, and go 0.1 mile. Turn left (south) onto GA 15, and go 2 miles. Turn right onto Country Road 10, and travel 5 miles to the campground.

About the campground: This campground overlooks Lake Rabun, and campers will enjoy views of the surrounding mountains as well. The campground offers a swimming area and hiking and fishing opportunities. The nearby towns of Clayton and Tallulah Falls, as well as Tallulah Gorge, make for interesting day trips, but with the scenery and activities available in the campground, you'll find it hard to leave for long.

43 Lake Russell

Location: About 3 miles southeast of Mt. Airy.
Sites: 42 tent/RV sites; maximum RV length 30 feet; no utilities; dump station and comfort stations with flush toilets, showers, and water on-site. Group camping area available by reservation only.
Fee per night: $$.
Season: Spring–fall.
Management: Chattahoochee-Oconee National Forest, Chattooga District, (706) 754–6221.
Finding the campground: From the intersection of GA 365/U.S. Route 23 and GA 197 west of Cornelia, go east on GA 197 for 2.6 miles. Turn right onto Dicks Hill Parkway, and go 0.7 mile. Turn left (southeast) onto Lake Russell Road, and travel 2.3 miles to the campground.

About the campground: Located in the scenic Lake Russell Wildlife Management Area, this campground offers lots of options for everyone. A swimming area, in-water slide, boat ramp, and fishing area will appeal to water lovers, and the nearby Ladyslipper Trail will appeal to hikers, mountain bikers, and equestrians. More trails are planned for the area, and this campground—already a favorite with the active crowd—will become more popular as more recreation options are developed. There is a special group area near the trailheads that is open by reservation only.

44 Black Rock Mountain State Park

Location: 3 miles northwest of Clayton.
Sites: 48 tent/RV sites with water and electricity; maximum RV length 30 feet; 11 walk-in campsites, no utilities; dump stations and comfort stations with flush toilets, showers, and coin laundry on-site. Group camping area available by reservation only.
Fee per night: $$$$.
Season: Year-round.
Management: Black Rock Mountain State Park, (706) 746–2141. Reservations: (800) 864–7275.
Finding the campground: From Clayton go north on U.S. Route 441 for 3 miles. Turn left at the directional sign in Mountain City. The road will end at the park.

About the campground: The drive up to Black Rock, the highest state park in Georgia, will set the tone for your visit: The winding road that climbs the mountain for which the park is named seems to be taking you high above and away from all your worldly cares. The vistas from the campground are worth quite a few pictures and reward the traveler with some spectacular colors in the fall. Besides the wonderful vistas, visitors can enjoy the 10-mile hiking trail system, picnic tables, and fishing and swimming at a seventeen-acre lake.

45 Tallulah Gorge State Park

Location: 0.5 mile north of Tallulah Falls.
Sites: 50 tent/RV sites with water and electricity, including 9 pull-throughs; maximum RV length 40 feet; dump stations and comfort stations with flush toilets, showers, and coin laundry on-site. Group camping area available by reservation only.
Fee per night: $$.
Season: Year-round.
Management: Tallulah Gorge State Park, (706) 754–7970. Reservations: (706) 754–7979.
Finding the campground: From Tallulah Falls go north on U.S. Route 441 for 0.5 mile. Just across the dam, turn right (east) onto Jane Hurt Yarn Road; the campground is on the right.

About the campground: Spectacular Tallulah Gorge is the focal point for this campground. The gorge, at about 2 miles long and almost 1,000 feet deep, is a scenic splendor. The park has a trail and several overlooks on the northeast rim of the gorge. Mountain bikers and hikers will enjoy a multiuse trail that takes you through the park and down to the shores of Tugalo Lake, at the lower end of the gorge. Non-bikers can enjoy Tallulah Falls Lake, just outside the campground. A boat ramp—convenient for anglers—picnic area, swimming beach, and playground offer plenty of opportunity for family fun. The town of Tallulah Falls has an interesting past as a tourist destination, and the Jane Hurt Yarn Interpretive Center in the park is a must-see for an informative exhibit on the local flora and fauna. Plan to spend a couple of days just seeing everything the park and surrounding area has to offer.

46 Willis Knob

Location: About 12 miles east of Clayton.
Sites: 8 tent/RV sites; maximum RV length 25 feet; no utilities; drinking water and flush toilets on-site.
Fee per night: $$.
Season: Year-round.
Management: Chattahoochee-Oconee National Forest, Tallulah District, (706) 782–3320.
Finding the campground: From Clayton go east on Warwoman Road for 11.5 miles. Turn right (south) onto Forest Road 157, and travel 2 miles to the campground.

About the campground: The Willis Knob and Rocky Gap horse trails make this campground extremely popular with equestrians. Facilities include twenty horse stalls. The campground is laid out in two loops, with a double campsite on each loop. If you don't travel by horseback but are lucky enough to stay at the campground, you can enjoy hiking on the Chattooga River Trail or fishing along the river and Warwoman Creek. Reservations for Willis Knob are required, so call at least fourteen days before you plan to make the trip.

Tugaloo State Park

47 Tugaloo State Park

Location: About 6 miles north of Lavonia.

Sites: 120 tent/RV sites with water and electricity, including 25 pull-throughs; maximum RV length 35 feet; dump station and comfort stations with flush toilets, showers, and coin laundry on-site. Group camping area available by reservation only.

Fee per night: $$$$.

Season: Year-round.

Management: Tugaloo State Park, (706) 356–4362. Reservations: (800) 864–7275.

Finding the campground: From Lavonia go north on GA 59 for 1 mile. Turn left (north) onto GA 328, and go 4.1 miles. Turn right (southeast) onto Tugaloo State Park Road, and travel 1 mile to the campground.

About the campground: Tugaloo, situated on a peninsula on Lake Hartwell, offers campers many sites right next to the water, and most have a good view of the lake. Largemouth bass fishing is a favorite local pastime, and the park offers a boat ramp. Campers can rent canoes and explore the surrounding lake. Tennis courts, volleyball courts, and horseshoe pits ensure that no one gets bored. The park also has a nature trail for quieter exercise.

The Piedmont Region

Located between the mountainous north part of the state and the southern plains, the Piedmont Region contains the greatest concentration of population in the state. Consisting mostly of rolling terrain, one of the highlights of the area is the number of lakes with varied recreation and entertainment opportunities. Many campsites are located in or near the metro Atlanta area, with all the conveniences and entertainment that such locations make possible. The area, like the rest of the state, is rich in history, including many Civil War sites and historic towns and cities that retain the charm of earlier days. Yet this is also the heart of a growing and vibrant center of social and economic importance for the region. Luckily, amid all the development, campers can still find plenty of great places to get away from it all.

West Point Lake Area

Stateline Campground

Location: 11 miles west of LaGrange.
Sites: 56 tent/RV sites with water and electricity; maximum RV length 40 feet; 66 tent sites, no utilities; dump stations and comfort stations with flush toilets, showers, and coin laundry on-site.
Fee per night: $$$.
Season: Spring–fall.
Management: U.S. Army Corps of Engineers, (706) 882–5439.
Finding the campground: From LaGrange go west on GA 109 for 10.7 miles. Turn left (south) onto Country Road 288, and travel 2.1 miles to the campground.

About the campground: Stateline has everything for the active camper. Those enjoying water sports and fishing will appreciate the boat ramp and sand swimming beach. The family will stay amused with a playground and hiking trails. The campground is laid out along the shores of the lake on several small points of land; most of the campsites are on or overlook the water and spaced apart enough for some peace and quiet.

Amity Campground

Location: 7 miles north of Lanett, Alabama.
Sites: 93 tent/RV sites with water and electricity; maximum RV length 40 feet; 3 tent sites, no utilities; dump stations and comfort stations with flush toilets, showers, and coin laundry on-site.
Fee per night: $$$.
Season: Spring–fall.
Management: U.S. Army Corps of Engineers, (334) 499–2404.

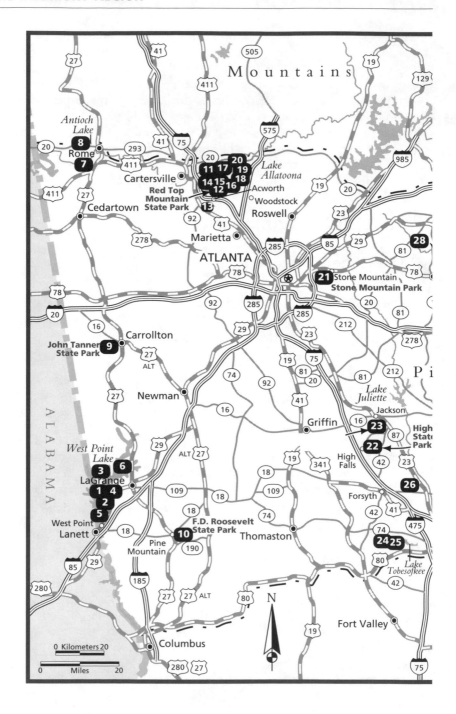

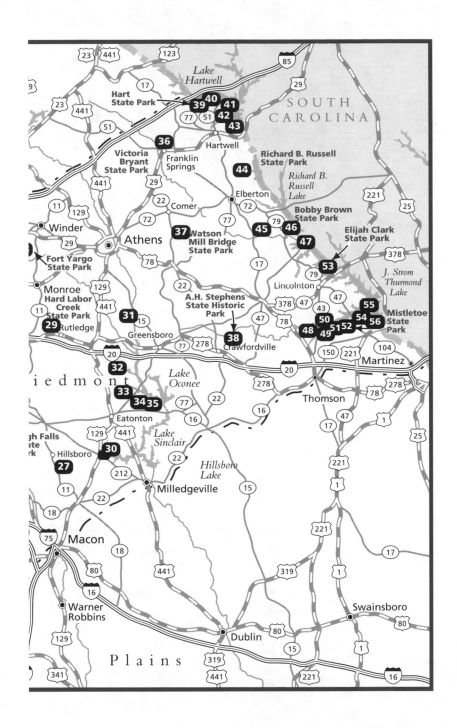

	Group sites	RV	Sites	Max. RV length	Hookups	Toilets	Showers	Coin laundry	Drinking water	Dump	Pets	Handicap access	Recreation	Fee	Season	Can reserve	Stay limit
1 Stateline	N	Y	122	40	WE	F	Y	Y	Y	Y	Y	Y	BFHLS	$$$	SP–FA	Y	14
2 Amity	N	Y	96	40	WE	F	Y	Y	Y	Y	Y	Y	BFHLS	$$$	SP–FA	Y	14
3 Holiday	N	Y	143	40	WE	F	Y	Y	Y	Y	Y	Y	BFHST	$$$	SP–FA	Y	14
4 Whitetail Ridge	N	Y	58	40	WE	F	Y	Y	Y	Y	Y	Y	BFHLS	$$$	SP–FA	Y	14
5 R. Scheafer Heard	N	Y	117	40	WE	F	Y	Y	Y	Y	Y	Y	BFLMST	$$$	SP–FA	Y	14
6 Lock and Dam	N	Y	31	40	WES	F	Y	Y	Y	Y	Y	Y	FHS	$$$		Y	14
7 Rocky Mountain	N	Y	48	40	WE	F	Y	N	Y	Y	Y	Y	BFHLS	$$		N	14
8 Ringer Park	N	Y	37	40		V	N	N	Y	N	Y	N	BFHLS	$$$	SP–FA	Y	14
9 John Tanner SP	Y	Y	31	40	WE	F	Y	Y	Y	Y	Y	Y	BFS	$$$$		Y	14
10 F. D. Roosevelt SP	Y	Y	140	40	WE	F	Y	Y	Y	Y	Y	Y	FHRS	$$$$		Y	14
11 McKaskey Creek	N	Y	51	35	WE	F	Y	Y	Y	Y	Y	Y	BFLS	$$$	SP–FA	Y	14
12 Red Top Mountain SP	Y	Y	92	40	WE	F	Y	Y	Y	Y	Y	Y	BFHLS	$$$$		Y	14
13 Old Highway 41	N	Y	50	40	WE	F	Y	Y	Y	Y	Y	Y	BFLS	$$$$	SP–FA	Y	14
14 McKinney	N	Y	150	40	WE	F	Y	Y	Y	Y	Y	Y	BFLS	$$$$		Y	14
15 Clark Creek North	N	Y	24	40	WE	F	Y	Y	Y	Y	Y	Y	BFS	$$$$	SP–FA	Y	14
16 Clark Creek South	N	Y	40	40	WE	F	Y	Y	Y	Y	Y	Y	BFLS	$$$$	SP–FA	Y	14
17 Upper Stamp Creek	N	Y	20	35		F	Y	N	Y	Y	Y	Y	BFLS	$$$$	SP–FA	Y	14
18 Payne	N	Y	39	40	WE	F	Y	Y	Y	Y	Y	Y	BFLS	$$$$	SP–FA	Y	14
19 Victoria	N	Y	72	40	WE	F	Y	Y	Y	Y	Y	Y	BFLS	$$$$	SP–FA	Y	14
20 Sweetwater	Y	Y	107	40	WES	F	Y	Y	Y	Y	Y	Y	BFHLS	$$$$	SP–FA	Y	14
21 Stone Mountain Park	N	Y	441	50	WES	F	Y	Y	Y	Y	Y	Y	BFGH LST	$$$$		Y	14
22 High Falls SP	Y	Y	112	50	WE	F	Y	Y	Y	Y	Y	Y	BFHLS	$$$$		Y	14
23 Indian Springs SP	Y	Y	88	50	WE	F	Y	Y	Y	Y	Y	Y	BFHLS	$$$$		Y	14
24 Claystone Park	N	Y	97	50	WE	F	Y	Y	Y	Y	Y	Y	BFLS			Y	14
25 Arrowhead Park	N	Y	76	50	WE	F	Y	N	Y	Y	Y	Y	BFLMS		SP–FA	Y	14
26 Dames Ferry	N	Y	78	50	WE	F	Y	N	Y	Y	Y	Y	BFLS	$$$$	SP–FA	Y	14
27 Hillsboro Lake	N	N	5			V	N	N	N	N	N	N	BFH			N	14
28 Fort Yargo SP	Y	Y	54	40	WE	F	Y	Y	Y	Y	Y	Y	BFHLMS	$$$$		Y	14
29 Hard Labor Creek SP	Y	Y	51	50	WE	F	Y	Y	Y	Y	Y	Y	BFGH HLMS	$$$$		Y	14
30 Lake Sinclair	N	Y	32	40		F	Y	N	Y	Y	Y	Y	BFHLMS	$$	SP–FA	Y	14
31 Oconee River	N	N	6			F	N	N	Y	N	Y	Y	BFS	$$		Y	14
32 Parks Ferry	Y	Y	103	50	WE	F	Y	Y	Y	Y	Y	Y	BFLS	$$$	SP–FA	Y	14
33 Old Salem	Y	Y	134	50	WE	F	Y	Y	Y	Y	Y	Y	BFLS	$$$	SP–FA	Y	14
34 Oconee Springs	N	Y	37	30	WE	F	Y	Y	Y	Y	Y	Y	BFLS	$$$	SP–FA	Y	14

	Group sites	RV	Sites	Max. RV length	Hookups	Toilets	Showers	Coin laundry	Drinking water	Dump	Pets	Handicap access	Recreation	Fee	Season	Can reserve	Stay limit
35 Lawrence Shoals	Y	Y	78	50	WE	F	Y	Y	Y	Y	Y	Y	BFHLS	$$$		Y	14
36 Victoria Bryant SP	Y	Y	25	40	WE	F	Y	Y	Y	Y	Y	Y	FGHMS	$$$$		N	14
37 Watson Mill Bridge SP	Y	Y	21	50	WE	F	Y	Y	Y	Y	Y	Y	BFHR	$$$$		Y	14
38 A. H. Stephens SHP	Y	Y	25	60	WE	F	Y	Y	Y	Y	Y	Y	BFHR	$$$$		Y	14
39 Hart SP	Y	Y	94	40	WE	F	Y	Y	Y	Y	Y	Y	BFHLMS	$$$$		Y	14
40 Paynes Creek	N	Y	44	50	WE	F	Y	Y	Y	Y	Y	Y	BFLS	$$$$		Y	14
41 Milltown	Y	Y	51	35	WE	F	Y	N	Y	Y	Y	Y	BFLS	$$$$		Y	14
42 Watsadler	N	Y	51	50	WE	F	Y	Y	Y	Y	Y	Y	BFL	$$$$		Y	14
43 Georgia River	N	N	10			F	N	N	Y		Y	Y	BF	$	SP–FA	N	14
44 Richard B. Russell SP	Y	Y	28	35	WE	F	Y	Y	Y	Y	Y	Y	BFHLS	$$$$		Y	14
45 Broad River	N	Y	31	50	WE	F	Y	N	Y	Y	Y	Y	BFL	$$$$		Y	14
46 Bobby Brown SP	Y	Y	61	35	WE	F	Y	Y	Y	Y	Y	Y	BFHLS	$$$$		Y	14
47 Hesters Ferry	N	Y	26	50	WE	F	Y	Y	Y	Y	Y	Y	BFLS	$$$$		Y	14
48 Big Hart	Y	Y	31	50	WE	F	Y	Y	Y	Y	Y	Y	BFHLS	$$$$		Y	14
49 Raysville	N	Y	55	40	WE	F	Y	Y	Y	Y	Y	Y	BFL	$$$$		Y	14
50 Clay Hill	N	Y	17	20	WE	F	Y	Y	Y	Y	Y	Y	BFL	$$$$		Y	14
51 Winfield	N	Y	80	35	WE	F	Y	N	Y	Y	Y	Y	BFLS	$$$$		Y	14
52 Mistletoe SP	Y	Y	92	70	WE	F	Y	Y	Y	Y	Y	Y	BFHLMS	$$$$		Y	14
53 Elijah Clark SP	Y	Y	165	40	WE	F	Y	N	Y	Y	Y	Y	BFHLMS	$$$$		Y	14
54 Wildwood Park	Y	Y	62	40	WE	F	Y	N	Y	Y	Y	Y	BFHLS	$$		Y	14
55 Ridge Road	N	Y	69	25	WE	F	Y	N	Y	Y	Y	Y	BFHLS	$$$$		Y	14
56 Petersburg	N	Y	93	50	WE	F	Y	N	Y	Y	Y	Y	BFHLS	$$$$		Y	14

Hookups: W = Water E = Electric S = Sewer **Toilets:** F = Flush V = Vault **Recreation:** B = Boating F = Fishing G = Golf H = Hiking L = Boat Launch M = Mountain Biking O = Off-Road Vehicles R = Horseback Riding S = Swimming T = Tennis **Fee:** $, less than $10; $$, $10–$15; $$$, $16–$20; $$$$, more than $20. **Maximum RV length** given in feet. **Stay limit** given in days. If no entry under **Season,** campgound is open all year. If no entry under **Fee,** camping is free.

Finding the campground: From Lanett, Alabama, travel north on Country Road 212 for 7 miles to the campground.

About the campground: West Point Lake lies on the Georgia/Alabama border. The lake is a favorite with anglers from around the region because of the great sportfishing opportunities available and is also popular with swimmers. Amity lies on the shores of the lake and offers the usual amenities, as well as a boat ramp and playground. Hiking trails offer some exercise options off water, and the scenery is pleasant and easy to enjoy.

Holiday Campground

Location: About 8 miles west of LaGrange.
Sites: 92 tent/RV sites with water and electricity; maximum RV length 40 feet; 51 tent sites, no utilities; dump stations and comfort stations with flush toilets, showers, and coin laundry on-site.
Fee per night: $$$.
Season: Spring–fall.
Management: U.S. Army Corps of Engineers, (706) 884–6818.
Finding the campground: From LaGrange travel west on GA 109 for 7.8 miles to the campground.

About the campground: Holiday is another West Point Lake campground for the active camper. The campground includes facilities for the anglers, swimmers, and other water-sports devotees. The landlubber can enjoy the playground and basketball and tennis courts. A hiking trail offers another form of exercise. The campsites are laid out along several small points jutting out into the lake, and most are right on or just above the water. The sites are well spaced.

Whitetail Ridge

Location: About 7 miles west of LaGrange.
Sites: 58 tent/RV sites with water and electricity; maximum RV length 40 feet; dump stations and comfort stations with flush toilets, showers, and coin laundry on-site.
Fee per night: $$$.
Season: Spring–fall.
Management: U.S. Army Corps of Engineers, (706) 884–8972.
Finding the campground: From LaGrange go west on GA 109 for 6.9 miles. Turn left (south) at the directional sign and travel 0.8 mile to the campground.

About the campground: Whitetail is named after the numerous deer native to the area, not the kid in the suntan lotion commercial. The campground has a boat ramp and facilities for boaters, anglers, and swimmers. There are more interior sites than at some of the other West Point Lake campgrounds, but these sites are just wooded enough to offer a nice mix of accessibility to the lake and privacy. Whitetail appears less developed than other nearby campgrounds, and other than the hiking trail on-site, caters mostly to the lake crowd.

5 R. Schaefer Heard

Location: 2 miles north of West Point.
Sites: 117 tent/RV sites with water and electricity, including 9 pull-throughs; maximum RV length 40 feet; dump stations and comfort stations with flush toilets, showers, and coin laundry on-site.
Fee per night: $$$.
Season: Spring–fall.

Management: U.S. Army Corps of Engineers, (706) 645–2404.
Finding the campground: From West Point go north on U.S. Route 29 for 1.9 miles. Turn left (west) at the directional sign, and follow the paved road to the campground.

About the campground: Located on the southern end of West Point Lake, Heard is another of the well-thought-out Corps campgrounds designed to offer a little of everything to the active camper. Naturally, the campground includes a boat ramp and lake access. Little campers will enjoy the playground, and bigger campers can fit a game of tennis in among the fishing, swimming, and other water sports. The campground is laid out on two peninsulas, with many sites enjoying lake views. The interior sites are pretty well wooded.

6 Ringer Park

Location: About 10 miles north of LaGrange.
Sites: 37 tent/RV sites, no utilities; maximum RV length 40 feet; vault toilets and water on-site.
Fee per night: $$$.
Season: Spring–fall.
Management: U.S. Army Corps of Engineers, (706) 645–2937.
Finding the campground: From LaGrange travel north on U.S. Route 27 for 9.8 miles. The campground is on the left.

About the campground: Located farther north and east than other campgrounds on West Point Lake, Ringer Park offers all of the same amenities. A boat ramp and facilities cater to the water lover and anglers. The kids can enjoy the playground and swimming in the lake, and families will enjoy the picnic area and hiking trails. Most sites are nicely wooded, and many are on the water. The campground is across the lake from the West Point Wildlife Management Area, so campers enjoy a little less visual reminder of the outside world.

Rome Area

7 Lock and Dam Park

Location: About 5 miles south of Rome.
Sites: 31 tent/RV sites with water, electricity, and sewer; maximum RV length 40 feet; dump stations and comfort stations with flush toilets, showers, and coin laundry on-site.
Fee per night: $$$.
Season: Year-round.
Management: Rome/Floyd County Parks and Recreation Authority, (706) 234–5001.
Finding the campground: From Rome go south on U.S. Route 27/441 for 3.5 miles. Turn right (west) onto Walker Mountain Road, and go 3.3 miles to Lock and

Dam Road. Turn right (north), and travel 0.2 mile; the campground is on the right.

About the campground: This campground is near the banks of the Coosa River, and eight of the campsites are actually next to the river, which is convenient for those who like to swim. Facilities include a trading post and bait shop. Fishing is also available from the lock. There is a playground for kids, as well as volleyball and horseshoe courts. Several short hiking trails and an observation tower offer lots of opportunities for exploration. The park is also building a small museum with live exhibits of local wildlife. Take a half day and visit nearby Cave Spring for some interesting sights.

8   Rocky Mountain Recreation Area

Location: About 15 miles northwest of Rome.
Sites: 39 tent/RV sites with water and electricity; maximum RV length 40 feet; 9 tent sites, no utilities; dump station and comfort stations with flush toilets and showers on-site.
Fee per night: $$.
Season: Year-round.
Management: Georgia Department of Natural Resources, (706) 802–5087.
Finding the campground: From Rome go north on U.S. Route 27 for 6.72 miles. Turn left onto Sykes/Storey Road, and go 0.1 mile. Turn left onto Big Texas Valley Road, and go 5 miles to the campground.

About the campground: Situated on 325-acre Antioch Lake, this campground offers something for everyone. A swimming beach and boat ramp cater to the water lovers in the crowd, and there is excellent fishing from the shore or boats. There are also 8 miles of hiking trails around the campground, with lots of options for different length hikes. Campsites are nicely spaced and wooded, offering good privacy. The campground also offers a group pavilion and shelter for larger groups.

John Tanner State Park

9   John Tanner State Park

Location: About 6 miles west of Carrollton.
Sites: 31 tent/RV sites with water and electricity, including 8 pull-throughs; maximum RV length 40 feet; dump stations and comfort stations with flush toilets, showers, and coin laundry on-site. Group camping area available by reservation only.
Fee per night: $$$$.
Season: Year-round.
Management: John Tanner State Park, (770) 830–2222. Reservations: (800) 864–7275.
Finding the campground: From Carrollton go west on GA 16 for 5.9 miles. Turn

left (southwest) onto Tanner Beach Road, and travel 0.5 mile to the campground.

About the campground: John Tanner State Park boasts the largest sand swimming beach of any state park in Georgia, and the park's two lakes offer something for almost every type of angler and water lover, including canoe and paddleboat rentals. Other activities include miniature golf, horseshoes, and a playground. The campsites are shaded and comfortable, and several overlook the lake.

F. D. Roosevelt State Park

10 F. D. Roosevelt State Park

Location: About 3 miles east of Pine Mountain.
Sites: 140 tent/RV sites with water and electricity, including 30 pull-throughs; maximum RV length 40 feet; dump stations and comfort stations with flush toilets, showers, and coin laundry on-site. Group camping area available by reservation only.
Fee per night: $$$$.
Season: Year-round.
Management: F. D. Roosevelt State Park, (706) 663–4858. Reservations: (800) 864–7275.
Finding the campground: From Pine Mountain go south on U.S. Route 27 for 0.5 mile. Turn left (east) onto GA 190 at the directional sign; follow GA 190 for 3 miles to the park entrance.

About the campground: Roosevelt, at 10,000 acres, is Georgia's largest state park. Campers will enjoy any one of a number of fun activities, including fishing on either of the park's two lakes. A swimming pool built by the Civilian Conservation Corps (CCC) during the depression offers campers a glimpse of the CCC's handiwork and craftmanship. The park offers guided hiking and horseback trips during the year, and nearby Warm Springs contains many historical points of interest regarding Franklin Roosevelt, who spent as much time here as he could during his presidency. Be sure to visit the Little White House, Roosevelt's vacation home. Nearby Callaway Gardens offers plenty of other diversions for all ages.

Lake Allatoona Area

11 McKaskey Creek

Location: About 3 miles east of Cartersville.
Sites: 32 tent/RV sites with water and electricity, including 2 pull-throughs; maximum RV length 35 feet; 19 tent sites, no utilities; dump stations and comfort stations with flush toilets, showers, and coin laundry on-site.
Fee per night: $$$.

Season: Spring–fall.
Management: U.S. Army Corps of Engineers, (770) 382–4700.
Finding the campground: From Cartersville go east on GA 20 for 1.5 miles, just east of the GA 20/I–75 exit. Turn right (south) onto Spur 20, and go 1.9 miles. Turn left (east) onto McKaskey Creek Road, which ends at the campground.

About the campground: McKaskey Creek is on the northwest corner of Lake Allatoona, which is still a little less developed than the southern shores of the lake. The campground includes some tent pads as well as regular tent/RV sites. A boat ramp, swimming area, and playground offer lots of opportunities for keeping the family busy, and the surroundings are pretty well suited to just doing nothing, if that's your thing. Fishing and boating are very popular on Lake Allatoona, and many lake-goers enjoy using the campgrounds as a base.

12 Red Top Mountain State Park

Location: About 6 miles north of Acworth.
Sites: 92 tent/RV sites with water and electricity, including 12 pull-throughs; maximum RV length 40 feet; dump stations and comfort stations with flush toilets, showers, and coin laundry on-site. Group camping area available by reservation only.
Fee per night: $$$$.
Season: Year-round.
Management: Red Top Mountain State Park, (770) 975–4226. Reservations: (800) 864–7275.
Finding the campground: From Acworth go north on I–75 to exit 285, Red Top Mountain Road. Turn right (east), and travel 2 miles to the park.

About the campground: Red Top Mountain is the only state park on Lake Allatoona and one of the few campgrounds on the lake open year-round. The facilities include two boat ramps, five fishing docks, a marina, and a swimming area; fishing and water sports are a favorite pastime for park visitors. For other entertainment, campers can enjoy the park's two excellent hiking/nature trails and the children's playground. The Red Top Mountain Lodge, in the park, includes a restaurant in case the fish aren't biting.

13 Old Highway 41 Campground

Location: About 1.5 miles northwest of Acworth.
Sites: 50 tent/RV sites with water and electricity, including 4 pull-throughs; maximum RV length 40 feet; dump station and comfort stations with flush toilets, showers, and coin laundry on-site.
Fee per night: $$$$.
Season: Spring–fall.
Management: U.S. Army Corps of Engineers, (770) 382–4700.
Finding the campground: From Acworth go north on GA 293/Main Street for 1.3 miles; the campground entrance is on the right.

About the campground: This is one of the older, more established campgrounds on Lake Allatoona. The sites are a little closer together, but many are next to the water and most offer pleasant lake views. Facilities include a boat ramp, separate picnic areas, and a playground for the junior campers. Swimming, fishing, and other water sports are the main focus of many campers here, and the campground offers a good opportunity to enjoy the lake. Acworth is very close by, with any modern conveniences one may desire.

14 McKinney Campground

Location: About 4 miles north of Acworth.
Sites: 150 tent/RV sites with water and electricity, including 25 pull-throughs; maximum RV length 40 feet; dump stations and comfort stations with flush toilets, showers, and coin laundry on-site.
Fee per night: $$$$.
Season: Year-round.
Management: U.S. Army Corps of Engineers, (770) 382–4700.
Finding the campground: From Acworth go north on Glade Road for 4 miles (or 3 miles from the Glade Road/I–75 exit). Turn left (west) onto Kings Camp Road, and travel 1 mile to the campground entrance.

About the campground: McKinney is one of several Corps of Engineer campgrounds on Lake Allatoona. The campground, like most Corps campgrounds, is laid out on a peninsula of land that juts out into the lake, with water on three sides. McKinney is one of the larger local campgrounds. Many of the campsites are right next to the water, and the interior sites are well wooded and spaced pleasantly far apart. Facilities include a boat ramp—convenient for boaters and anglers—swimming, beach, and picnic area. The campground is close enough to Acworth for any midtrip needs that may arise, and Red Top Mountain State Park is just a few miles away.

15 Clark Creek North

Location: About 3 miles north of Acworth.
Sites: 24 tent/RV sites with water and electricity, including 2 pull-throughs; maximum RV length 40 feet; dump stations and comfort stations with flush toilets, showers, and coin laundry on-site.
Fee per night: $$$$.
Season: Spring–fall.
Management: U.S. Army Corps of Engineers, (770) 382–4700.
Finding the campground: From Acworth travel north on Glade Road for 2.9 miles. The campground entrance is on the left.

About the campground: The two Clark Creek campgrounds are located on the more populous southern part of Lake Allatoona. The drive to the campgrounds doesn't inspire that "getting away from it all" feeling because of the local development. The campground itself is very nice and feels somewhat isolated and private, with wooded campsites that are well spaced and comfortable. Many sites overlook the lake. The campground's central location offers anglers and boaters easy access to the rest of the lake.

6 Clark Creek South

Location: About 3 miles north of Acworth.
Sites: 24 tent/RV sites with water and electricity; maximum RV length 40 feet; 16 tent sites, no utilities; dump station and comfort station with flush toilets, showers, and coin laundry on-site.
Fee per night: $$$$.
Season: Spring–fall.
Management: U.S. Army Corps of Engineers, (770) 382–4700.
Finding the campground: From Acworth travel north on Glade Road for 2.7 miles; the campground entrance is on the right.

About the campground: See Clark Creek North. Additionally, Clark Creek South offers a boat ramp and a swimming area for campers' use. Most sites are well spaced and wooded, and several overlook the lake. Some sites are paired closer together than others. These offer a good option for friends/cocampers to be closer than normal sites would allow.

7 Upper Stamp Creek

Location: About 3.5 miles east of Cartersville.
Sites: 18 tent/RV sites; maximum RV length 35 feet; 2 tent sites, no utilities; dump station and comfort station with flush toilets and showers on-site.
Fee per night: $$$$.
Season: Spring–fall.
Management: U.S. Army Corps of Engineers, (770) 382–4700.
Finding the campground: From the intersection of GA 20 and I–75 east of Cartersville, go east on GA 20 for 4.8 miles. Turn right (southeast) onto Wilderness Camp Road, and travel 1.9 miles to the campground.

About the campground: Upper Stamp Creek is located on the less-developed north side of Lake Allatoona. As a result, campers enjoy more of a feeling of removal from the nearby suburbs and can relax and enjoy the pleasures of the lake. This is one of the smaller Corps campgrounds, but the sites are reasonably wooded and well spaced. Several sites are right on the water. A boat ramp and swimming area cater to water lovers, and fishing is a favorite local pursuit.

18 Payne Campground

Location: About 4 miles northeast of Acworth.
Sites: 39 tent/RV sites with water and electricity, including 3 pull-throughs; maximum RV length 40 feet; dump station and comfort stations with flush toilets, showers, and coin laundry on-site.

Fee per night: $$$$.
Season: Spring–fall.
Management: U.S. Army Corps of Engineers, (770) 382–4700.
Finding the campground: From the intersection of I–75 and GA 92 in Acworth, go north on GA 92 for 1 mile. Turn left (north) onto Kellogg Creek Road. Travel 2.8 miles; the campground is on the right.

About the campground: Payne is located on the eastern end of the lake, which is also well developed and mostly suburbs. The campground is located on a peninsula that juts out into the lake, offering many sites with good views and access to the water. Most sites are wooded and pretty private. Facilities include a boat ramp, swimming area, and playgrounds for the kiddies. The campground offers good access to the lake for anglers and boaters.

19 Victoria

Location: About 6 miles northwest of Woodstock.
Sites: 72 tent/RV sites with water and electricity, including 8 pull-throughs; maximum RV length 40 feet; dump station and comfort stations with flush toilets, showers, and coin laundry on-site.
Fee per night: $$$$.
Season: Spring–fall.
Management: U.S. Army Corps of Engineers, (770) 382–4700.
Finding the campground: From the intersection of I–575 and GA 205 (Bells Ferry Road), go north on GA 205 for 6.3 miles. Turn left (west) onto Victoria Road, and go 1.6 miles. Turn right (west) onto Victoria Landing Drive, and travel 1 mile to the campground entrance on the left.

About the campground: Don't let the drive to Victoria fool you. Although the campground appears to be in the heart of suburbia, like most Corps campgrounds, the site is well located and large enough so that campers feel like they are somewhat isolated from the rest of the world. The campground sits on several small peninsulas, offering many waterside campsites and nicely wooded interior sites. Boating and fishing are the major attractions of the lake, and the campground offers a swimming area and nearby boat ramp to accommodate aquatically minded campers.

20 Sweetwater Campground

Location: About 11 miles east of Cartersville.
Sites: 105 tent/RV sites with water and electricity, including 10 pull-throughs; 2 tent/RV sites with water, electricity, and sewer; maximum RV length 40 feet; dump station and comfort stations with flush toilets, showers, and coin laundry on-site. Group camping area available by reservation only.
Fee per night: $$$$.
Season: Spring–fall.
Management: U.S. Army Corps of Engineers, (770) 382–4700.
Finding the campground: From the intersection of GA 20 and I–75 east of

Cartersville, go east on GA 20 for 10.8 miles. Turn right (southeast) on Fields Chapel Road, and follow the signs to the campground.

About the campground: Sweetwater Creek is one of the larger Corps campgrounds, but the layout and thoughtful design of the area doesn't give one the impression of a large campground. Many of the sites are wooded, and all are well spaced. Some overlook or are next to the water, which is great for anglers, and there are some paired sites for multicamper groups. Facilities include a boat ramp, swimming area, and playgrounds located near some campsites to offer the camping family some entertainment for the young'uns. There are several unmarked trails along the lakeshore for the adventurous hiker. The campground adjoins a wildlife management area, so there's plenty of room to wander.

Stone Mountain Park

21 Stone Mountain Park

Location: 1 mile east of Stone Mountain.
Sites: 144 tent/RV sites with water, sewer, and electricity, including 18 pull-throughs; 297 tent sites with water and electricity; maximum RV length 50 feet; dump station and comfort stations with flush toilets, showers, and coin laundry on-site.
Fee per night: $$$$.
Season: Year-round.
Management: Stone Mountain Park, (770) 498–5690.
Finding the campground: From the intersection of I–285 and U.S. Route 78 on the east side of Atlanta, travel east on U.S. Route 78 for 7.8 miles to the park entrance.

About the campground: If you're looking for something to keep everyone in the family busy, Stone Mountain Park is your answer. Stone Mountain is one of the world's largest exposed granite outcroppings. Visit the antebellum museum; take a riverboat cruise; enjoy the championship golf courses; take a train ride around the mountain; take the skylift to the top of the mountain; and view the world's largest carving, the confederate memorial, on the side of the mountain. In other words, there's plenty to do here. The campsites are a little closer together than most public campgrounds, but the attractions of the park are the big draw here, and you'll likely spend most of your time enjoying the many entertaining options available, including tennis, hiking, and fishing. The campground includes a boat ramp, swimming area, and playground.

Forsyth and Macon Area

22 High Falls State Park

Location: About 0.5 mile east of High Falls.

Sites: 112 tent/RV sites with water and electricity, including 20 pull-throughs; maximum RV length 50 feet; dump station and comfort stations with flush toilets, showers, and coin laundry on-site. Group camping area available by reservation only.
Fee per night: $$$$.
Season: Year-round.
Management: High Falls State Park, (912) 993–3053. Reservations: (800) 864–7275.
Finding the campground: From the intersection of I–75 and High Falls Road, travel east for 1.8 miles. The park entrance is on the left.

About the campground: High Falls State Park lies among the remains of an early nineteenth-century town. The foundations of the old gristmill still remain, and the waterfalls and the lake make for some great scenery. Fishing is easy from the many spots along the river or from the lakeshore or boat (a boat launch is on-site). Three hiking trails, two playgrounds, a pool, and miniature golf offer something for everyone in the family. The campground is split into two sections: one on the lake and the other along the banks of the river. Be sure to visit nearby Dauset Trails Nature Center and the Jarrell Plantation for day trips kids of all ages will love.

23 Indian Springs State Park

Location: About 4.5 miles south of Jackson.
Sites: 88 tent/RV sites with water and electricity; maximum RV length 50 feet; dump station and comfort stations with flush toilets, showers, and coin laundry on-site. Group camping area available by reservation only.
Fee per night: $$$$.
Season: Year-round.
Management: Indian Springs State Park, (770) 504–2277. Reservations: (800) 864–7275.
Finding the campground: From Jackson go south on U.S. Route 23/GA 42 for 4.5 miles. Turn right (southwest) on GA 42, and travel 2 miles; the park is on the right.

About the campground: Indian Springs is named after a natural spring long used by Native Americans for the water's healing properties. A former resort town in the nineteenth century, some of the old buildings' remains are still visible along the highway. The present park, one of the oldest state parks in the county, was built by the Civilian Conservation Corps during the Depression. Facilities/activities include a 105-acre lake with boat ramp, swimming area, miniature golf, fishing- and paddleboat rentals, and hiking. Be sure to visit the on-site museum for a glimpse into the area's past. The campground itself sits in two sections along the shores of the lake, and many sites overlook the water. The campground is located away from the springs area of the park, which gets the most day use, so campers can enjoy the peaceful surroundings.

24 Claystone Park (Lake Tobesofkee)

Location: About 3 miles west of Macon.
Sites: 97 tent/RV sites with water and electricity, including 8 pull-throughs; maxi-

mum RV length 50 feet; dump station and comfort station with flush toilets, showers, and coin laundry on-site.

Fee per night: $$$.

Season: Year-round.

Management: Bibb County Parks and Recreation, (478) 474–8770.

Finding the campground: From the intersection of GA 74 and I–475 west of Macon, go west on GA 74 for 1.1 miles. Turn left (southwest) onto Mosely Dixon Road, and travel 1.9 miles; the campground entrance is on the left.

About the campground: Lake Tobesofkee is Macon's playground, with fishing and water sports taking top honors on the "to-do" list. The campground is relatively new and modern, and sites are reasonably well spaced, though not heavily wooded. Several sites are near the water. The campground offers a boat ramp and swimming area, and a nearby marina serves boaters' needs. A wide sand swimming beach, playground, and picnic area on-site cater to the little ones.

25 Arrowhead Park (Lake Tobesofkee)

Location: About 3 miles west of Macon.

Sites: 76 tent/RV sites with water and electricity; maximum RV length 50 feet; dump station and comfort stations with flush toilets and showers on-site.

Fee per night: $$.

Season: Spring–fall.

Management: Bibb County Parks and Recreation, (478) 474–8770.

Finding the campground: From the intersection of I–475 and U.S. Route 80, go west on U.S. Route 80 for 3.6 miles. Turn right onto Tidwell Road, and go 0.3 mile. Turn left onto Columbus Road, and go 0.25 mile to the entrance sign on the right. Turn right and follow the road to the campground entrance.

About the campground: Arrowhead, on the south side of Tobesofkee, is a little older than Claystone, its neighbor to the north. Sites are well spaced, though not especially wooded, and all offer either lake views or access. There is a boat ramp for anglers and boaters and a swimming area in the park, as well as picnic areas and a pavilion. Two playgrounds serve the little ones. New recreational trails are being built in the park, which will make it a popular destination for mountain bikers and others from the area.

26 Dames Ferry Park (Lake Juliette)

Location: About 10 miles east of Forsyth.

Sites: 78 tent/RV sites with water and electricity; maximum RV length 50 feet; dump station and comfort stations with showers and flush toilets on-site.

Fee per night: $$$$.

Season: Spring–fall.

Management: Georgia Power Company, (912) 994–7945.

Finding the campground: From the intersection of I–75 and GA 18 in Forsyth, go east on GA 18 for 10.9 miles. Turn left (north) onto U.S. Route 23/GA 87, and travel 1.4 miles to the campground entrance on the left.

About the campground: Lake Juliette is somewhat different from most man-made lakes in Georgia in that the shores are not developed. Campers will enjoy the seeming isolation of the area; other than anglers on the lake, there's not a lot going on to attract large numbers of visitors. The result is a campground that allows ample opportunity to enjoy the peace and quiet of the surroundings. The campsites are reasonably well wooded and offer good separation from other sites. A boat ramp and swimming beach are next to the campground.

Hillsboro Lake

Hillsboro Lake

Location: About 3 miles east of Hillsboro.
Sites: 5 tent sites; no utilities; vault toilets on-site.
Fee per night: None.
Season: Year-round.
Management: Chattahoochee-Oconee National Forest, Oconee District, (706) 485–7110.
Finding the campground: From GA 11 in Hillsboro, at the directional sign go southeast for 3 miles on a paved county road to the campground.

About the campground: Hillsboro is the smallest of the Forest Service campgrounds in Georgia. It offers plenty of relaxation, pleasant surroundings, and hiking, and anglers and boaters will enjoy the location on the lake. All sites are next to the water. Take some time to visit the nearby historical towns of Monticello and Eatonton.

Fort Yargo State Park

Fort Yargo State Park

Location: About 1 mile south of Winder.
Sites: 47 tent/RV sites with water and electricity, including 5 pull-throughs; maximum RV length 40 feet; 7 walk-in tent sites; dump station and comfort stations with flush toilets, showers, and coin laundry on-site. Group camping area by reservation only.
Fee per night: $$$$.
Season: Year-round.
Management: Fort Yargo State Park, (770) 867–3489.
Finding the campground: From Winder go south on GA 81 for 1 mile; the park is on the left.

About the campground: Fort Yargo is directly in the path of a growing metro Atlanta, but the park itself offers a feeling of well-insulated distance from the surrounding development. The campground is located on a dead-end road with no through traffic. The lake offers lots of opportunities for bank fishing and swimming, and boat and canoe rentals are available at the park. (There is an on-site boat launch.) The campsites are wooded, and several are located along the lakeshore. A playground offers entertainment for the little ones, and several campsites are located next to the playground for family campers. A mountain bike and hiking trail circles the lake and offers access to the old log fort for which the park is named. The park's proximity to civilization belies its quiet setting.

Hard Labor Creek State Park

29 Hard Labor Creek State Park

Location: About 2 miles north of Rutledge.
Sites: 51 tent/RV sites with water and electricity, including 8 pull-throughs; maximum RV length 50 feet; dump station and comfort stations with flush toilets, showers, and coin laundry on-site. Group camping area available by reservation only.
Fee per night: $$$$.
Season: Year-round.
Management: Hard Labor Creek State Park, (706) 557–3001. Reservations: (800) 864–7275.
Finding the campground: From Rutledge go north on Fairplay Road for 2 miles to the park entrance.

About the campground: At more than 5,000 acres, Hard Labor Creek is one of the larger state parks in Georgia. A favorite attraction at the park is the eighteen-hole golf course, and golfers from around the area come here to enjoy the course's challenge. Campsites are nicely spaced and wooded, and amenities at the campground include a boat launch for anglers and boaters, swimming beach, playground, and canoe and paddleboat rentals. Hiking trails offer even more recreation options. The camping in this park is the same consistently good experience as at most state parks, and the added option of golf makes it a great destination for the duffer-camper.

Lake Sinclair and Lake Oconee Area

30 Lake Sinclair

Location: About 12 miles south of Eatonton.
Sites: 17 tent/RV sites; maximum RV length 40 feet; 15 tent sites, no utilities; dump station and comfort stations with drinking water, flush toilets, and showers on-site.
Fee per night: $$.
Season: Spring–fall.
Management: Chattahoochee/Oconee National Forest, (706) 485–7110.
Finding the campground: From Eatonton go south on U.S. Route 129 for 11 miles.

Turn left (east) onto GA 212 and go 1 mile. Turn left (east) onto Twin Bridges Road (Forest Road 1062), and go 1.1 miles. Turn left (north) onto Putnam Beach Road, and follow it to the campground.

About the campground: Located on the shores of Lake Sinclair, the focus for most visitors is the excellent fishing and boating opportunities that the lake offers. Facilities include a boat ramp and swimming area. Like most national forest campgrounds, the sites are laid out along smaller loops, with some wooded sites and some sites along the lakeshore. A hiking and mountain biking trail offers a chance to exercise the legs, and the surroundings and laid-back atmosphere offers campers the opportunity to enjoy a nice escape from everyday hurries.

Oconee River Campground

Location: About 12 miles northwest of Greensboro.
Sites: 6 tent sites, no utilities; flush toilets and drinking water on-site.
Fee per night: $$.
Season: Year-round.
Management: Chattahoochee/Oconee National Forest, Oconee District, (706) 485–7110.
Finding the campground: From Greensboro go north on GA 15 for 12.1 miles to the campground entrance.

About the campground: Located on the banks of the Oconee River, this campground offers plenty of opportunity to enjoy the topography of the piedmont. The low hills and slow-moving rivers and streams offer campers a place to let the cares of the world slide away. Campsites are reasonably well separated and wooded, and some sit along the river. The fishing is said to always be pretty good in these parts, and there's also a picnic area. Take time to enjoy the 1 mile hike to nearby Skull Shoals Historic Area to get a glimpse of bygone days.

Parks Ferry (Lake Oconee)

Location: About 7 miles southwest of Greensboro.
Sites: 53 tent/RV sites with water and electricity, including 9 pull-throughs; maximum RV length 50 feet; 50 tent sites, no utilities; dump station and comfort station with flush toilets, showers, and coin laundry on-site. Group camping area available by reservation only.
Fee per night: $$$.
Season: Spring–fall.
Management: Georgia Power Company, (706) 453–4308.
Finding the campground: From the intersection of I–20 and GA 44 south of Greensboro, go south on GA 44 for 5.3 miles. Turn right (northwest) onto Carey Station Road, and go 3.9 miles to a directional sign at a paved road. Turn left (south), and travel 1 mile to the campground.

About the campground: Parks Ferry offers lake-goers and anglers another great option for enjoying Lake Oconee. The campground sits on the shores of one of the narrower sections of the lake, and the surrounding terrain offers pleasant views. Most sites are wooded or shaded, and several are situated along the lakeshore. Lake facilities include a boat ramp and swimming area. There is a playground in the campground to entertain the little campers and a field for games and such.

33 Old Salem (Lake Oconee)

Location: About 11.5 miles south of Greensboro.
Sites: 99 tent/RV sites with water and electricity, including 22 pull-throughs; maximum RV length 50 feet; 35 tent sites, no utilities; dump station and comfort stations with flush toilets, showers, and coin laundry on-site. Group camping area available by reservation only.
Fee per night: $$$.
Season: Spring–fall.
Management: Georgia Power Company, (706) 467–2850.
Finding the campground: From the intersection of I–20 and GA 44 south of Greensboro, go south on GA 44 for 8.5 miles. Turn left (south) on Linger Longer Road, and go 0.5 mile to a directional sign and paved road on the right. Turn right (south), and travel 1 mile to the campground.

About the campground: Old Salem offers lake lovers another good way to enjoy Lake Oconee. The campground is on a peninsula that offers campers many sites by the water, as well as wooded interior sites. Facilities include a boat ramp and swimming area. There are several nice spots along the bank for fishing. A playground offers entertainment for little campers, and the campground's surroundings offer plenty of opportunity for relaxation.

34 Oconee Springs Park (Lake Oconee)

Location: About 11 miles east of Eatonton.
Sites: 37 tent/RV sites with water and electricity; maximum RV length 30 feet; dump station and comfort stations with flush toilets, showers, and coin laundry on-site.
Fee per night: $$$.
Season: Spring–fall.
Management: Oconee Springs Park, (706) 485–8423.
Finding the campground: From Eatonton go east on GA 16 for 10.2 miles to Oconee Springs Road. Turn right (south), and travel 1.4 miles. Turn right (southeast) on Rockville Road, and follow it to the campground.

About the campground: At twelve acres, Oconee Springs is a relatively small campground, but the sites are well spaced, and several are located along the lakeshore. Fishing, boating, and swimming are favorites on Lake Oconee, and the campground has some nice fishing spots along the shore. A playground and horseshoe pits offer onshore entertainment, and the on-site store offers limited supplies and groceries in case you forget something. There is also an on-site boat launch.

35 | Lawrence Shoals (Lake Oconee)

Location: About 13 miles east of Eatonton.
Sites: 53 tent/RV sites with water and electricity; maximum RV length 50 feet; 25 tent sites, no utilities; dump station and comfort stations with flush toilets, showers, and coin laundry on-site. Group camping area available by reservation only.
Fee per night: $$$.
Season: Year-round.
Management: Georgia Power Company, (706) 485–5494.
Finding the campground: From Eatonton go east on GA 16 for 13.7 miles. Turn left (north) onto Wallace Dam Road, and follow the signs to the campground.

About the campground: Lawrence Shoals offers campers a pleasant opportunity to take advantage of the popular fishing and water sports on Lake Oconee. The campground sits on the shores of the lake and offers a boat ramp, swimming area, and dock for lake-goers. A playground, recreation field, horseshoe pits, and nature trail offer off-water diversions when the fishing's not great. Most sites are reasonably well wooded, and several are next to the water.

Athens Area

36 | Victoria Bryant State Park

Location: About 1 mile north of Franklin Springs.
Sites: 25 tent/RV sites with water and electricity, including 8 pull-throughs; maximum RV length 40 feet; dump station and comfort station with flush toilets, showers, and coin laundry on-site. Group camping area available by reservation only.
Fee per night: $$$$.
Season: Year-round.
Management: Victoria Bryant State Park, (706) 245–6270. Reservations: (800) 864–7275.
Finding the campground: From Franklin Springs go north on GA 327 for 1 mile; the park entrance is on the left.

About the campground: Though this campground is relatively small, the lucky campers who stay here will not want for something to do. Besides enjoying the beauty of the park itself, campers can choose from a swimming pool, two stocked fishing ponds (one for campers only and one for disabled persons only), three playgrounds for the kids, a nine-hole golf course and driving range, and a 5-mile perimeter mountain bike and hiking trail. There is also a shorter nature trail with wildlife feeding areas along the way, so take your camera.

Watson Mill Bridge State Park

Location: 3 miles south of Comer.
Sites: 21 tent/RV sites with water and electricity, including 18 pull-throughs; maximum RV length 50 feet; dump station and comfort station with flush toilets, showers, and coin laundry on-site. Group camping area available by reservation only.
Fee per night: $$$$.
Season: Year-round.
Management: Watson Mill Bridge State Park, (706) 783–5349. Reservations: (800) 864–7275.
Finding the campground: From Comer go south on GA 22 for 3 miles to park entrance.

About the campground: The focus of this park is the 229-foot-long Watson Mill Bridge, the longest covered bridge in Georgia still on its original site. Besides the obvious interest and picturesque beauty of the bridge and park surroundings, campers can also enjoy fishing in the millpond, canoe and paddleboat rentals, and a nature trail. For the more adventurous, equestrian and hiking trails are also available. In this park just enjoying the surroundings is an activity itself.

A. H. Stephens State Historic Park

Location: In Crawfordville.
Sites: 25 tent/RV sites with water and electricity, including 10 pull-throughs; maximum RV length 60 feet; dump station and comfort stations with flush toilets, showers, and coin laundry on-site. Group camping area available by reservation only.
Fee per night: $$$$.
Season: Year-round.
Management: A. H. Stephens State Historic Park, (706) 456–2602.
Finding the campground: The park entrance is in Crawfordville, 2 miles north of I–20.

About the campground: This park is named after Alexander H. Stephens, vice president of the Confederacy and governor of Georgia. Liberty Hall, Stephens's home, is located at the front of the park and is open for tours. The adjoining Confederate museum houses a fine collection of Civil War artifacts. The campground is located toward the rear of the park and offers campers access to two fishing lakes, and fishing- and paddleboat rentals. A playground is located within the campground, and equestrian and hiking trails round out the many options to keep campers entertained.

Lake Hartwell Area

39 Hart State Park

Location: About 3 miles northwest of Hartwell.
Sites: 78 tent/RV sites with water and electricity, including 30 pull-throughs; max-

imum RV length 40 feet; 16 walk-in tent sites, no utilities; dump station and comfort stations with flush toilets, showers, and coin laundry on-site. Group camping area available by reservation only.
Fee per night: $$$$.
Season: Year-round.
Management: Hart State Park, (706) 376–8756. Reservations: (800) 864–7275.
Finding the campground: From Hartwell go east on U.S. Route 29 North for 1 mile. Turn left (north) onto Ridge Road, and travel 1 mile to the park entrance.

About the campground: Located on the shores of beautiful Lake Hartwell, Hart offers much for the water-oriented. A boat ramp, fishing docks, and swimming beach cater to those enjoying the lake, and fishing is one of the major attractions for visitors. The campground is located on the shores of the lake, and most sites are nicely wooded and by or near water. Other interests include a multiuse trail and seasonal music programs at the Cricket Theatre.

0 Paynes Creek

Location: About 8.5 miles north of Hartwell.
Sites: 44 tent/RV sites with water and electricity, including 31 pull-throughs; maximum RV length 50 feet; dump station and comfort station with flush toilets, showers, and coin laundry on-site.
Fee per night: $$$$.
Season: Year-round.
Management: U.S. Army Corps of Engineers, (706) 856–0300.
Finding the campground: From Hartwell go north on GA 51 for 6.8 miles. Turn left (northwest) onto Country Road 301, and travel 5 miles to the campground.

About the campground: If you want a waterfront campsite, try Paynes Creek; thirty-seven of the forty-four sites are on the water. All sites are nicely wooded and separated from each other, and all offer at least a view of Lake Hartwell, the major draw. The campground offers a boat ramp for anglers and boaters and a swimming area for campers' use. A playground is located within the campground for entertaining the little ones.

1 Milltown

Location: About 7 miles northeast of Hartwell.
Sites: 51 tent/RV sites with water and electricity; maximum RV length 35 feet; dump station and comfort stations with drinking water, flush toilets, and showers on-site. Group camping area available by reservation only.
Fee per night: $$$$.
Season: Year-round.
Management: U.S. Army Corps of Engineers, (706) 856–0300.
Finding the campground: From Hartwell go north on GA 51 for 4 miles. Turn right (east) on New Prospect Road, and go 4 miles. Turn at the directional sign, and follow it to the campground entrance.

About the campground: Besides the usual beauty of Lake Hartwell, Milltown offers a somewhat unique option for larger camping groups: Three smaller loops within the campground with seven to ten sites each can be reserved separately for use by larger groups. The loops contain campsites just like the regular campground and are basically smaller sections that can be gated off. What better way to enjoy camping with your friends and family than by having your own section of the campground? Of course the campground includes the usual lakeside activities/amenities, such as swimming, fishing, a boat ramp, and a playground for keeping the kids occupied.

Watsadler

Location: About 5 miles east of Hartwell.
Sites: 51 tent/RV sites with water and electricity, including 18 pull-throughs; maximum RV length 50 feet; dump station and comfort station with flush toilets, showers, and coin laundry on-site.
Fee per night: $$$$.
Season: Year-round.
Management: U.S. Army Corps of Engineers, (706) 856–0300.
Finding the campground: From Hartwell go east on U.S. Route 29N for 4.5 miles; the campground entrance is on the left.

About the campground: Watsadler is located on the southern end of Lake Hartwell, near the dam, and the wide expanse of the water makes for some great sunrises and sunsets. Just about every site in this campground is next to the water. Double sites are also available for groups with more than two tents or one RV. Facilities include a boat ramp, fishing dock, and playground. Like most Corps campgrounds, just about every site here is a good one.

Georgia River Recreation Area

Location: About 5.5 miles east of Hartwell.
Sites: 10 tent sites, no utilities; flush toilets available on-site.
Fee per night: $.
Season: Spring–fall.
Management: U.S. Army Corps of Engineers, (877) 444–6777.
Finding the campground: From Hartwell go east on U.S. Route 29N for 5 miles. The campground is on the left before you cross the river.

About the campground: Georgia River is located right on the Savannah River just below the front of the dam. Trout are stocked in the river for anglers, and fishing is a favorite pastime here. The primitive sites are closer together than some other area campgrounds, but this campground is mostly surrounded by woods. Hartwell is close by, with good restaurants and anything else campers might need. If you want to be near the lake but get more of a "woodsy" feeling, try Georgia River.

Richard B. Russell State Park

44 Richard B. Russell State Park

Location: About 9 miles northeast of Elberton.
Sites: 28 tent/RV sites with water and electricity, including 6 pull-throughs; maximum RV length 35 feet; dump station and comfort stations with flush toilets, showers, and coin laundry on-site. Group camping area available by reservation only.
Fee per night: $$$$.
Season: Year-round.
Management: Richard B. Russell State Park, (706) 213–2045. Reservations: (800) 864–7275.
Finding the campground: From Elberton go north on GA 77 for 1.3 miles. Turn right (east) onto Ruckersville Road, and travel 8 miles to the park entrance.

About the campground: Richard B. Russell is located on Richard B. Russell Lake and offers campers plenty of facilities to enjoy. The campground is one of the newer ones in Georgia's state parks, and most sites are next to or overlook the lake. Sites are well spaced and somewhat private. The boat ramp, canoe and paddleboat rentals, swimming area, and rowing area offer water lovers plenty to choose from. Other activities/amenities include fishing, a nature trail, and hiking and biking trails.

J. Strom Thurmond Lake and Richard B. Russell Lake Area

45 Broad River (J. Strom Thurmond Lake)

Location: About 17.5 miles southeast of Elberton.
Sites: 31 tent/RV sites with water and electricity, including 15 pull-throughs; maximum RV length 50 feet; dump station and comfort stations with flush toilets and showers on-site.
Fee per night: $$$$.
Season: Year-round.
Management: U.S. Army Corps of Engineers, (706) 359–2053.
Finding the campground: From Elberton go south on GA 17 for 2 miles. Turn left (east) onto GA 72 and go 10.7 miles. Turn right (south) onto GA 79, and go 9.8 miles to the campground.

About the campground: This campground is located on the Broad River area of Thurmond Lake. The fishing in these parts is considered some of the best in the country, and this campground is a favorite of anglers and boaters alike. A boat ramp serves the campground. The surroundings are pleasantly rural, and the atmosphere is very laid-back. This campground features double and even some triple campsites for larger families or small groups that want to camp close to each other.

46 | Bobby Brown State Park (Richard B. Russell Lake)

Location: About 20 miles southeast of Elberton.
Sites: 61 tent/RV sites with water and electricity, including 7 pull-throughs; maximum RV length 35 feet; dump station and comfort stations with flush toilets, showers, and coin laundry on-site. Group camping area available by reservation only.
Fee per night: $$$$.
Season: Year-round.
Management: Bobby Brown State Park, (706) 213–2046. Reservations: (800) 864–7275.
Finding the campground: From Elberton go east on GA 72 for 10.8 miles. Turn right (south) onto Bobby Brown State Park Road, and go 9 miles to the campground.

About the campground: This campground is also located on Richard B. Russell Lake and offers plenty of opportunity for enjoyment of the water with a boat ramp, dock, swimming area, and pool. Fishing boats, canoes, and paddleboats are available for rent. Campsites are nicely located mostly next to the lake and are spaced well. The surroundings are great for relaxation if you're not into fishing and water sports. Campers can also enjoy almost 2 miles of hiking trails and the scenic views along the lakeshore.

47 | Hesters Ferry (J. Strom Thurmond Lake)

Location: About 11 miles north of Lincolnton.
Sites: 16 tent/RV sites with water and electricity, including 6 pull-throughs; 10 tent sites, no utilities; maximum RV length 50 feet; dump station and comfort stations with flush toilets, showers, and coin laundry on-site.
Fee per night: $$$$.
Season: Year-round.
Management: U.S. Army Corps of Engineers, (706) 359–2746.
Finding the campground: From Lincolnton go north on GA 79 for 11.9 miles. Turn right (east) on GA 44 and go 2 miles. Turn right (east) at the directional sign and follow the road to the campground.

About the campground: Hesters Ferry is located on what many locals consider the best fishing area on Thurmond Lake. The tent sites are located on a separate loop, and all campsites are next to the water. Facilities include a boat ramp and swimming area. This campground offers anglers and water-sports fans a pleasant place to enjoy the lake.

48 | Big Hart (J. Strom Thurmond Lake)

Location: About 9.5 miles north of Thomson.
Sites: 24 tent/RV campsites with water and electricity, including 15 pull-throughs; 7 tent sites, no utilities; maximum RV length 50 feet; dump station and comfort station with flush toilets, showers, and coin laundry on-site. Group camping area available by reservation only.

Fee per night: $$$$.
Season: Year-round.
Management: U.S. Army Corps of Engineers, (706) 595–6759.
Finding the campground: From the intersection of I–20 and U.S. Route 78 (exit 172) north of Thomson, go north on U.S. Route 78 for 8 miles. Turn right (east) onto Russell Landing Road to the campground.

About the campground: Big Hart is located at the confluence of Big Creek and Hart Creek, on the western end of J. Strom Thurmond Lake. The campground is relatively small but includes a group tent area, which can accommodate thirty campers. Campers enjoy activities/facilities such as fishing, hiking, a boat ramp, swimming beach, and playground at the Big Hart Recreation Area, next to the campground. Most sites are well spaced and fairly shaded, with nice views of the water.

9 Raysville (J. Strom Thurmond Lake)

Location: About 10 miles north of Thomson.
Sites: 55 tent/RV sites with water and electricity, including 4 pull-throughs; maximum RV length 40 feet; dump station and comfort station with flush toilets, showers, and coin laundry on-site.
Fee per night: $$$$.
Season: Year-round.
Management: U.S. Army Corps of Engineers, (706) 595–6759.
Finding the campground: From the intersection of I–20 and U.S. Route 78 (exit 172) north of Thomson, go north on U.S. Route 78 for 3 miles. Turn right (east) onto GA 43 and go 4.8 miles; the campground is on the left.

About the campground: Raysville, like nearby Big Hart, is on the western end of J. Strom Thurmond Lake. The campground offers campers access to the many recreation options available on the lake. The lake is the primary focus of this campground, and besides the boat ramp and comfort station there are few other facilities. Sites are reasonably well spaced and shaded, and the campground offers pleasant surroundings to while away the postfishing hours.

0 Clay Hill (J. Strom Thurmond Lake)

Location: About 8.5 miles south of Lincolnton.
Sites: 10 tent/RV sites with water and electricity; maximum RV length 20 feet; 7 tent sites, no utilities; dump station and comfort stations with flush toilets, showers, and coin laundry on-site.
Fee per night: $$$$.
Season: Year-round.
Management: U.S. Army Corps of Engineers, (706) 359–7495.
Finding the campground: From Lincolnton go south on GA 43 for 7.9 miles. Turn left (east) onto Clay Hill Road, and go 1.8 miles to the campground.

About the campground: Clay Hill sits on a peninsula, so many sites offer direct views of the water. The campground is small but offers campers lake access via a boat ramp. Fishing is a local favorite here. The smaller campground usually makes for a quieter camping experience than one finds with some of the larger campgrounds. Sites are well spaced and shaded.

Winfield (J. Strom Thurmond Lake)

Location: About 14.5 miles northeast of Thomson.
Sites: 73 tent/RV sites with water and electricity; maximum RV length 35 feet; 7 tent sites, no utilities; dump station and comfort stations with flush toilets, showers, and coin laundry on-site.
Fee per night: $$$$.
Season: Year-round.
Management: U.S. Army Corps of Engineers, (706) 541–0147.
Finding the campground: From the intersection of I–20 and GA 150 (exit 175) northeast of Thomson, go north on GA 150 for 5.8 miles. Turn left (north) at the directional sign onto the paved county road, and follow it to the campground.

About the campground: Winfield is located on the western section of Thurmond Lake. Many sites are located near the water, and the surroundings are pleasant enough, even without the lake. Water sports, swimming, and fishing are the big draws here, and you'll find many campers bring their boats along for the trip. The campground includes a boat ramp. Mistletoe State Park is nearby and offers other recreation options (see Mistletoe State Park).

Mistletoe State Park (J. Strom Thurmond Lake)

Location: About 14.5 miles northeast of Thomson.
Sites: 92 tent/RV sites with water and electricity, including 22 pull-throughs; maximum RV length 70 feet; dump station and comfort stations with flush toilets, showers, and coin laundry on-site. Group camping area available by reservation only.
Fee per night: $$$$.
Season: Year-round.
Management: Mistletoe State Park, (706) 541–0321. Reservations: (800) 864–7275.
Finding the campground: From the intersection of I–20 and GA 150 (exit 175) north of Thomson, go north on GA 150 for 7.5 miles. Turn left (north) at the directional sign onto Mistletoe Park Road, which dead-ends at the park entrance.

About the campground: Mistletoe is located on the western section of J. Strom Thurmond Lake and is known as one of the best spots for bass fishing in the region. The campground is located on a peninsula, and most sites are on or in direct view of the water. Many campers bring boats, and most sites' proximity to the water adds convenience. Facilities/activities include a boat ramp; fishing dock; playground; some excellent nature, hiking, and bike trails with wildlife viewing areas; and swimming. If you like spotting deer, Mistletoe is a good bet; the park seems full of them.

53 Elijah Clark State Park (J. Strom Thurmond Lake)

Location: About 7 miles northeast of Lincolnton.
Sites: 165 tent/RV sites with water and electricity, including 68 pull-throughs; maximum RV length 40 feet; dump station and comfort stations with flush toilets and showers on-site. Group camping area available by reservation only.
Fee per night: $$$$.
Season: Year-round.
Management: Elijah Clark State Park, (706) 359–3458. Reservations: (800) 864–7275.
Finding the campground: From Lincolnton go northeast on U.S. Route 378 for 7 miles to the park entrance.

About the campground: The campground at Elijah Clark is one of the larger ones in the state. Though there are a lot of sites, they are still reasonably well spaced and offer decent privacy. Thurmond Lake is one of the biggest draws to this park, and you'll see lots of anglers, swimmers, and others enjoying water sports all around the campground. Facilities include boat ramps, a nature trail, a playground, and miniature golf. Be sure to check out the log cabin museum that details the history of the area.

54 Wildwood Park (J. Strom Thurmond Lake)

Location: About 16 miles northwest of Martinez.
Sites: 52 tent/RV sites with water and electricity, including 2 pull-throughs; maximum RV length 40 feet; 10 tent sites, no utilities; dump station and comfort stations with flush toilets and showers on-site. Group camping area available by reservation only.
Fee per night: $$.
Season: Year-round.
Management: Wildwood Park, (706) 541–0586.
Finding the campground: From Martinez go north on GA 104 for 14.5 miles to the intersection of GA 47 and GA 150 at Pollard's Corner. Continue north on GA 47 for 1.6 miles to the campground entrance.

About the campground: Wildwood has something both for the water lover and for other active folks. A 4.5-mile hiking trail offers a chance to take in the local scenery. More ambitious hikers can hike sections of the nearby Bartram Trail. Wildwood also has a boat ramp, sand swimming beach, and playground. The campground is laid out in two loops, with sites spread out among the wooded area. Sites are a little closer than the norm but are reasonably well screened and offer some relaxing surroundings. Many of the sites are right on the water, which is convenient for anglers who can't wait to try their luck.

55 Ridge Road (J. Strom Thurmond Lake)

Location: About 17.5 miles northwest of Martinez.

Sites: 63 tent/RV sites with water and electricity, including 20 pull-throughs; 6 tent sites, no utilities; maximum RV length 25 feet; dump station and comfort stations with flush toilets and showers on-site.
Fee per night: $$$$.
Season: Year-round.
Management: U.S. Army Corps of Engineers, (706) 541–0282.
Finding the campground: From Martinez go northwest on GA 104 (Washington Road) for 16.8 miles. Turn right (east) onto Ridge Road, and travel 4.8 miles to the campground.

About the campground: Ridge Road was one of the first campgrounds on Thurmond Lake. The sites are well spaced and nicely shaded, and many offer excellent views of the water. The tent sites are separated on their own little peninsula, giving them a more isolated feel. Activities/facilities include fishing, hiking, a boat ramp, swimming area, and playground. The area surrounding the campground is relatively undeveloped, and the little ones will enjoy the common appearance of deer around and in the campground.

56 Petersburg (J. Strom Thurmond Lake)

Location: About 14.5 miles northwest of Martinez.
Sites: 85 tent/RV sites with water and electricity, including 55 pull-throughs; 8 tent sites, no utilities; maximum RV length 50 feet; dump station and comfort stations with flush toilets and showers on-site.
Fee per night: $$$$.
Season: Year-round.
Management: U.S. Army Corps of Engineers, (706) 541–9464.
Finding the campground: From Martinez go northwest on GA 104 for 14.5 miles. Turn right (east) onto U.S. Route 221 and go 2 miles. Turn left onto Country Road 64 and go 0.9 mile to the campground.

About the campground: Petersburg is one of the larger Corps campgrounds on Thurmond Lake. The campground offers lots of opportunities to enjoy the water, including a boat ramp, fishing dock, and two swimming areas. A hiking trail offers dry entertainment, and nearby Lake Springs Recreation Area has more beaches and two playgrounds. The nearby Thurmond Dam and Visitor Center offers a nice side trip for curious campers. Campsites are very well spaced, especially some of the sites surrounding the smaller inlets of the lake. Campers seeking privacy will be well pleased with Petersburg.

The Plains Region

The Plains Region is where campers can still find the taste and feel of another time in the state's history. This region is the largest and most rural in the state, stretching from the foothills of the piedmont to the lowlands of the coast. Campers and travelers should take their time here; there's a whole different state from the bustling north waiting to be discovered. Many of this area's campgrounds are located at places of historic significance. Campers will find that much of the past has been preserved here, and there are lots of opportunities to learn about "the way things used to be." There are several large recreational lakes in the region as well, so sportspersons and water lovers won't feel left out. Camping is a year-round activity here, and most campgrounds are open all year long. Take some time to discover the hidden charms of the Plains Region; you won't be disappointed.

Lake Walter F. George Area

1 Florence Marina State Park

Location: About 16 miles west of Lumpkin.
Sites: 43 tent/RV sites with water and electricity, including 20 pull-throughs; maximum RV length 50 feet; dump station and comfort stations with flush toilets, showers, and coin laundry on-site. Group camping area available by reservation only.
Fee per night: $$$$.
Season: Year-round.
Management: Florence Marina State Park, (912) 838–6870. Reservations: (800) 864–7275.
Finding the campground: From Lumpkin go west on GA 39C for 16 miles; the park is at the intersection of GA 39C and GA 39.

About the campground: For water lovers and anglers, Florence Marina offers great access, including a boat launch, to Lake Walter F. George. The park even has a marina and lighted fishing pier. The clubhouse adjacent to the campground offers a swimming pool and tennis courts, and the Kirbo Interpretive Center offers campers an opportunity to learn some of the varied history of the area. Campsites are well spaced, though not overly wooded. The campground is centrally located and offers good access to all the park facilities.

2 Rood Creek

Location: About 16 miles west of Lumpkin.
Sites: 12 tent/RV sites; no utilities; maximum RV length 20 feet; vault toilets available on-site.
Fee per night: None.
Season: Spring–fall.
Management: U.S. Army Corps of Engineers, (912) 768–2516. Reservations: (800) 444–6777.

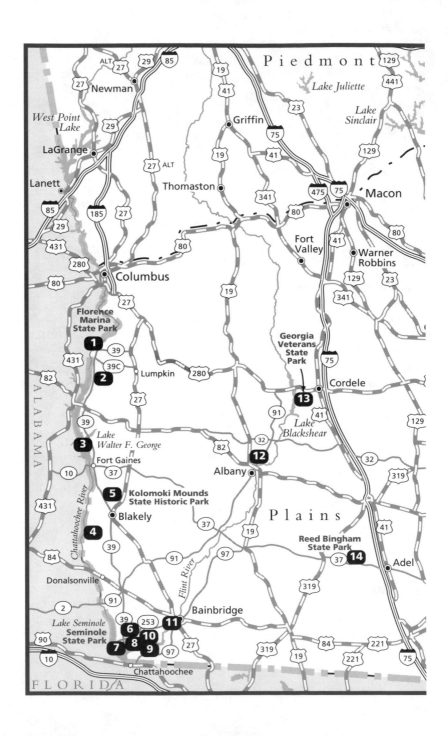

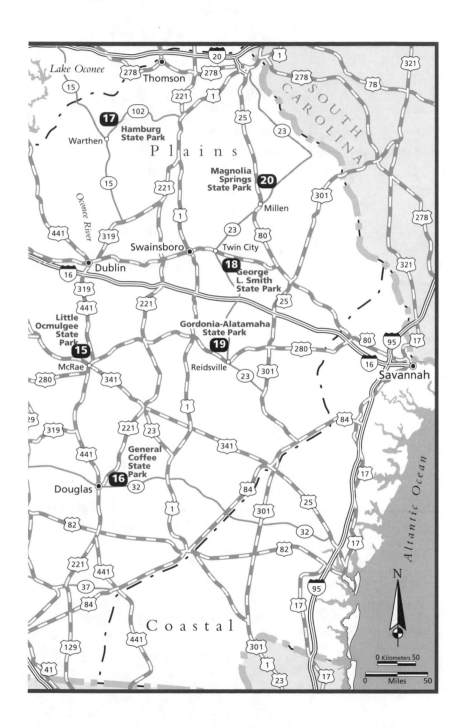

	Group sites	RV	Sites	Max. RV length	Hookups	Toilets	Showers	Coin laundry	Drinking water	Dump	Pets	Handicap Access	Recreation	Fee	Season	Can reserve	Stay limit
1 Florence Marina SP	Y	Y	43	50	WE	F	Y	Y	Y	Y	Y	Y	BFLMST	$$$$		Y	14
2 Rood Creek	N	Y	12	20		V	N	N	N	N	N	N	BFL		SP–FA	N	14
3 Cotton Hill	N	Y	114	40	WE	F	Y	Y	Y	Y	Y	Y	BFL	$$$		Y	14
4 Coheelee Creek	N	N	14			V	N	N	N	N	N	N	BFL			N	14
5 Kolomoki Mounds SHP	N	Y	43	50	WE	F	Y	Y	Y	Y	Y	Y	BFHS	$$$$		Y	14
6 Seminole SP	Y	Y	50	50	WE	F	Y	Y	Y	Y	Y	Y	BFHLS	$$$$		Y	14
7 East Bank	N	Y	70	50	WE	F	Y	Y	Y	Y	Y	Y	BFHLS	$$$		Y	14
8 River Junction	N	Y	16	50		F	Y	N	Y	N	Y	Y	BFL	$		N	14
9 Faceville Landing	N	N	6			V	N	N	N	N	Y	N	BFL			N	14
10 Hales Landing	N	N	14			F	Y	N	Y	N	Y	N	BFL	$		N	14
11 Earl May	N	Y	10	35	WE	F	Y	N	Y	Y	Y	N	BFHL	$		N	14
12 Chehaw Park	N	Y	47	50	WE	F	Y	N	Y	Y	Y	Y	FHM	$$		N	14
13 Georgia Veterans SP	Y	Y	77	50	WE	F	Y	Y	Y	Y	Y	Y	BFGHLS	$$$$		Y	14
14 Reed Bingham SP	Y	Y	46	60	WE	F	Y	Y	Y	Y	Y	Y	BFH	$$$$		Y	14
15 Little Ocmulgee SP	Y	Y	55	50	WE	F	Y	Y	Y	Y	Y	Y	BFGST	$$$$		Y	14
16 Hamburg SP	Y	Y	30	50	WE	F	Y	Y	Y	Y	Y	Y	BFH	$$$$		Y	14
17 General Coffee SP	Y	Y	50	60	WE	F	Y	Y	Y	Y	Y	Y	BFH	$$$$		Y	14
18 George L. Smith SP	Y	Y	25	40	WE	F	Y	Y	Y	Y	Y	Y	BFH	$$$$		Y	14
19 Gordonia-Alatamaha SP	N	Y	23	35	WE	F	Y	Y	Y	Y	Y	Y	BFGST	$$$$		Y	14
20 Magnolia Springs SP	Y	Y	26	50	WE	F	Y	Y	Y	Y	Y	Y	BFHS	$$$$		Y	14

Hookups: W = Water E = Electric S = Sewer **Toilets:** F = Flush V = Vault **Recreation:** B = Boating F = Fishing G = Golf H = Hiking L = Boat Launch M = Mountain Biking O = Off-Road Vehicles R = Horseback Riding S = Swimming T = Tennis **Fee:** $, less than $10; $$, $10–$15; $$$, $16–$20; $$$$, more than $20. **Maximum RV length** given in feet. **Stay limit** given in days. If no entry under **Season**, campgound is open all year. If no entry under **Fee**, camping is free.

Finding the campground: From Lumpkin go west on GA 39C for 16 miles. Turn left (south) onto GA 39 and go 3 miles. Turn right onto a dirt county road at the directional sign; the dirt road ends at the campground.

About the campground: Rood Creek is the only Corps primitive campground on the Georgia side of Lake Walter F. George. The sites are spaced along the creek and give easy access to the lake. For anglers who just want the basics for a fishing camping trip, Rood Creek is the perfect answer. A boat ramp serves boaters, and there are many good fishing spots along the shore as well. The campground feels very isolated, a result of its location at the end of a dirt county road.

3 Cotton Hill

Location: About 9 miles north of Fort Gaines.
Sites: 104 tent/RV sites with water and electricity, including 10 pull-throughs; maximum RV length 40 feet; 10 tent sites with water; dump station and comfort stations with flush toilets, showers, and coin laundry on-site.
Fee per night: $$$.
Season: Year-round.
Management: U.S. Army Corps of Engineers, (229) 768–3061.
Finding the campground: From Fort Gaines go north on GA 39 for 9 miles; the campground entrance is on the left.

About the campground: Cotton Hill offers boaters and anglers another good reason to visit Lake Walter F. George. The campground sits on a peninsula jutting out into the lake, and almost all of the sites are next to the water. The tent sites are nicely located closest to the larger part of the lake. Facilities include a boat ramp and dock, two playgrounds, and a group shelter.

Blakely Area

Coheelee Creek

Location: About 11 miles southwest of Blakely.
Sites: 14 tent sites; no utilities; vault toilets available on-site.
Fee per night: None.
Season: Year-round.
Management: Early County, (229) 723–4238.
Finding the campground: From Blakely go southeast on GA 62 for 9.4 miles. Turn right (southeast) onto Old River Road. Travel 1.3 miles to the park entrance on the left.

About the campground: If you want just the basics, this is your spot. Situated along one of the feeder creeks to the Chattahoochee River, this campground is set up for anglers. There are no utilities, but picnic tables along the creek offer a nice place for a meal, and the boat ramp offers river access. Be sure to walk back up to the covered bridge, a well-preserved example of those that used to be found throughout the area.

Kolomoki Mounds State Historic Park

Location: About 6 miles north of Blakely.
Sites: 43 tent/RV sites with water and electricity, including 16 pull-throughs; maximum RV length 50 feet; dump station and comfort stations with flush toilets, showers, and coin laundry on-site.
Fee per night: $$$$.
Season: Year-round.

Management: Kolomoki Mounds State Historic Park, (229) 724–2150. Reservations: (800) 864–7275.

Finding the campground: From Blakely go north 1 mile on U.S. Route 27. Turn left (north) at the directional sign onto Kolomoki Park Road and follow it about 5 miles to the park entrance.

About the campground: The seven mounds within the park are historically and archeologically fascinating, and the excellent museum and the mounds themselves will keep curious campers occupied for quite a while. Campsites are well spaced, though not heavily wooded. Other facilities include two swimming pools, two lakes for fishing, a boat dock, nature trails, and miniature golf. The park also has fishing boats for rent.

Lake Seminole Area

Seminole State Park

Location: About 16 miles south of Donalsonville.
Sites: 50 tent/RV sites with water and electricity, including 43 pull-throughs; maximum RV length 50 feet; dump station and comfort stations with flush toilets, showers, and coin laundry on-site. Group camping area available by reservation only.
Fee per night: $$$$.
Season: Year-round.
Management: Seminole State Park, (229) 861–3137. Reservations: (800) 864–7275.
Finding the campground: From Donalsonville go south on GA 39 for 16 miles. Turn left (east) onto GA 253; the park entrance is just across the bridge.

About the campground: This park sits on the northern part of Lake Seminole, an excellent fishing and water sports destination for the entire region. Campsites are reasonably well spaced, though not particularly wooded. Facilities include boat ramps and a fishing dock, swimming beach, miniature golf, a playground, and a gift shop on-site. The educational 2-mile Gopher Tortoise Trail gives campers great insight into the varied local wildlife habitat.

East Bank

Location: About 1 mile north of Chattahoochee, Florida.
Sites: 65 tent/RV sites with water and electricity; maximum RV length 50 feet; 4 tent sites and 1 handicapped site, no utilities; dump station and comfort stations with flush toilets, showers, and coin laundry on-site.
Fee per night: $$$.
Season: Year-round.
Management: U.S. Army Corps of Engineers, (229) 662–9273.
Finding the campground: From Chattahoochee, Florida, go north on Booster Club Road for 1 mile. Turn left (west) onto East Bank Road and follow it to the campground.

About the campground: East Bank is the southernmost campground on Lake Seminole in Georgia. Several sites are beside or very close to the lakeshore. Most sites are well spaced, though not particularly wooded. Campground facilities/activities include a boat ramp, fishing dock, playground, horseshoe pits, volleyball courts, a nature trail, and swimming. Campers will have plenty to do here, or they can just lay back and enjoy the surroundings.

River Junction

Location: About 3 miles north of Chattahoochee, Florida.
Sites: 16 tent/RV sites; no utilities; maximum RV length 50 feet; comfort station with flush toilets and showers on-site.
Fee per night: $.
Season: Year-round.
Management: U.S. Army Corps of Engineers, (229) 662–2001.
Finding the campground: From Chattahoochee, Florida, go north on Booster Club Road for 2 miles. Turn left (northwest) at the directional sign, and follow the road to the campground.

About the campground: River Junction offers anglers and those partial to water sports a no-frills way to enjoy Lake Seminole. The sites have no utilities, but the comfort stations on-site make tent camping seem almost civilized. Campsites have good access to the water, and the campground has a boat ramp and small dock. If you plan to spend most of your time on the water, this is a great place to start.

Faceville Landing

Location: About 10 miles southwest of Bainbridge.
Sites: 6 tent sites; no utilities; vault toilets on-site.
Fee per night: None.
Season: Year-round.
Management: U.S. Army Corps of Engineers, (229) 662–2001.
Finding the campground: From Bainbridge go southwest on GA 97 for 13 miles. Turn right (north) onto Faceville Landing Road, and travel 2.1 miles to the campground entrance.

About the campground: Faceville offers no-frills camping for those who wish to enjoy the pleasures of Lake Seminole. The campground has no facilities except a boat ramp and picnic shelter. There are some nice fishing spots along the lakeshore. This park is a favorite for anglers, and its relatively small size usually means a quieter camping experience.

Hales Landing

Location: About 5.8 miles southwest of Bainbridge.
Sites: 14 tent sites; no utilities; 1 site handicapped accessible; comfort station with flush toilets and showers on-site.

Fee per night: $.
Season: Year-round.
Management: U.S. Army Corps of Engineers, (229) 662–2001.
Finding the campground: From the intersection of U.S. Route 84 and GA 253 northwest of Bainbridge, go southeast on GA 253 for 3.6 miles. Turn left (south) onto Ten Mile Still Road, and travel 2 miles; the campground entrance is on the left.

About the campground: Another of the no-frills Corps campgrounds on Lake Seminole, Hales Landing is near the northeastern end of the lake and closest to Bainbridge. Though the sites do not have utilities, the comfort station offers enough luxury to make utilityless camping comfortable and easy. The campground has a boat ramp with small dock—great for boaters and anglers—a picnic area, and a group shelter. Sites are reasonably well spaced.

11 Earl May Boat Basin

Location: In Bainbridge.
Sites: 10 tent/RV sites with water and electricity; maximum RV length 35 feet; dump station and comfort stations with flush toilets and showers on-site.
Fee per night: $.
Season: Year-round.
Management: City of Bainbridge, (229) 248–2010.
Finding the campground: Located near the intersection of Shotwell Street and the Bainbridge Bypass (GA 84).

About the campground: Earl May is located on the Flint River, a few miles away from Lake Seminole. Its location offers excellent access to the lake for boaters. Two of the sites are next to the river, with the rest a short walk away. Amenities include a sand swimming beach, boat ramp, picnic tables, and pavilions. A recently completed 3.5-mile paved path through the surrounding countryside and a 0.5-mile boardwalk offer lots of opportunities to view the local flora and fauna. Young and old campers alike will enjoy the old steam engine that sits near the campground. Sports and activity fields add to the diversity of the park.

South-Central Georgia

12 Chehaw Wild Animal Park

Location: About 1.5 miles northeast of Albany.
Sites: 47 tent/RV sites with water and electricity, including 17 pull-throughs; maximum RV length 50 feet; dump station and comfort stations with flush toilets and showers on-site.
Fee per night: $$.
Season: Year-round.
Management: Chehaw Wild Animal Park, (229) 430–5275.
Finding the campground: From the intersection of GA 91 and U.S. Route 19/82

on the north side of town, go northeast on GA 91 for 1.2 miles to the park entrance.

About the campground: The campsites at Chehaw are reasonably spaced and decently wooded, and facilities include a huge playground for the little ones and fishing in Lake Chehaw. But chances are you'll spend lots of time in the Chehaw Wild Animal Park next to the campground. Campers of all ages can enjoy a drive-through safari, visit other animal and habitat exhibits, and enjoy miles of hiking and biking trails. There is enough to do in the park to keep campers of all ages busy for more than one visit.

13 Georgia Veterans State Park

Location: 8.5 miles west of Cordele.
Sites: 77 tent/RV sites with water and electricity, including 40 pull-throughs; maximum RV length 50 feet; dump station and comfort stations with flush toilets, showers, and coin laundry on-site. Group camping area available by reservation only.
Fee per night: $$$$.
Season: Year-round.
Management: Georgia Veterans State Park, (229) 276–2371. Reservations: (800) 864–7275.
Finding the campground: From Cordele go west on U.S. Route 280 for 8.5 miles to the park entrance.

About the campground: History buffs will enjoy Georgia Veterans, a park dedicated to U.S. military veterans of all wars. The park includes both indoor and outdoor museums with enough military hardware and memorabilia to keep campers of all ages fascinated for quite some time. As if that weren't enough, campers can also enjoy an eighteen-hole golf course, fishing and boating (there's an on-site boat launch) on Lake Blackshear, a nature trail, and a swimming pool and swimming beach. This campground truly offers something for campers of all ages.

14 Reed Bingham State Park

Location: About 6 miles west of Adel.
Sites: 46 tent/RV sites with water and electricity, including 23 pull-throughs; maximum RV length 60 feet; dump station and comfort stations with flush toilets, showers, and coin laundry on-site. Group camping area available by reservation only.
Fee per night: $$$$.
Season: Year-round.
Management: Reed Bingham State Park, (229) 896–3551. Reservations: (800) 864–7275.
Finding the campground: From the intersection of I–75 and GA 37 (exit 39), go west on GA 37 for 6 miles to the park entrance.

About the campground: This park's focus is on the natural surroundings and habitat of the Plains Region. The park surrounds a 375-acre lake, and fishing, boating, and water sports are local favorites. The park has two nature trails: the 0.5-mile Gopher Tortoise Nature Trail and the Coastal Plains Nature Trail. Both trails are excellent interpretive experiences that offer a rare study of the local, fast-disappearing natural habitat. Campsites are nicely spaced and wooded and offer plenty of privacy.

15 Little Ocmulgee State Park

Location: About 2 miles north of McRae.
Sites: 55 tent/RV sites with water and electricity, including 12 pull-throughs; maximum RV length 50 feet; dump station and comfort stations with flush toilets, showers, and coin laundry on-site. Group camping area available by reservation only.
Fee per night: $$$$.
Season: Year-round.
Management: Little Ocmulgee State Park, (229) 868–7474. Reservations: (800) 864–7275.
Finding the campground: From McRae go north on U.S. Route 319/441 for 2 miles to the park entrance.

About the campground: Little Ocmulgee is another of the Georgia parks built by the Civilian Conservation Corps in the late 1930s and early 1940s. This park opened in 1940. Facilities/activities include a lake and swimming beach, conference center, lodge and restaurant, eighteen-hole golf course, tennis courts, playgrounds, group shelters, fishing, and boating. This is a great family or large-group destination, and campers can enjoy as much (or as little) of the park as they wish at their leisure.

16 General Coffee State Park

Location: About 6 miles east of Douglas.
Sites: 50 tent/RV sites with water and electricity, including 50 pull-throughs; maximum RV length 60 feet; dump station and comfort stations with flush toilets, showers, and coin laundry on-site. Group camping area available by reservation only.
Fee per night: $$$$.
Season: Year-round.
Management: General Coffee State Park, (912) 384–7082. Reservations: (800) 864–7275.
Finding the campground: From Douglas go east on GA 32 for 6 miles to the park entrance.

About the campground: Nature and history lovers will enjoy this park. Highlights include a cypress swamp and nature trail, and lots of rare and endangered plant and animal species for sharp-eyed campers to spot. History buffs will enjoy the Heritage Farm, a restored homestead with log cabins and other buildings and structures of the period, farm animals, and educational exhibits on the ways of life in the old days. A lake offers lots of fishing and boating opportunities. Campsites are reasonably well spaced, though not particularly heavily wooded.

Hamburg State Park

17 Hamburg State Park

Location: About 6 miles north of Warthen.
Sites: 30 tent/RV sites with water and electricity, including 7 pull-throughs; maximum RV length 50 feet; dump station and comfort station with flush toilets, showers, and coin laundry on-site. Group camping area available by reservation only.
Fee per night: $$$$.
Season: Year-round.
Management: Hamburg State Park, (478) 552–2393. Reservations: (800) 864–7275.
Finding the campground: From Warthen go north on GA 102 for 1.5 miles. Turn left (north) onto Hamburg Road, and travel 4 miles to the park entrance.

About the campground: Hamburg is the site of a 1921 gristmill, which is still in operation today. A museum exhibits old agricultural tools and implements used in the area earlier in the twentieth century. The campsites are nicely spaced and wooded and are close to the lake, which offers some excellent fishing. Campers can rent canoes and paddleboats. A nature trail offers a glimpse of some of the natural habitat that was here before modern man. The park is somewhat off the beaten path and offers campers a more isolated and quiet atmosphere to enjoy the surroundings.

Southeast Georgia

18 George L. Smith State Park

Location: About 4 miles southeast of Twin City.
Sites: 25 tent/RV sites with water and electricity, including 6 pull-throughs; maximum RV length 40 feet; dump station and comfort stations with flush toilets, showers, and coin laundry on-site. Group camping area available by reservation only.
Fee per night: $$$$.
Season: Year-round.
Management: George L. Smith State Park, (912) 763–2759. Reservations: (800) 864–7275.
Finding the campground: From Twin City go south on GA 23 for 3.4 miles. Turn left (northeast) onto George L. Smith Park Road, and travel 1.8 miles to the park entrance.

About the campground: The quiet enjoyment of the pristine natural surroundings makes a camping trip to this park a great experience. History buffs will appreciate the old gristmill, covered bridge, and millpond (which also happens to be a great place to fish). Boat rentals are available at the park. Campsites are nicely spaced and wooded, and the park enhances the natural beauty of the surroundings with hiking trails and a playground for families.

9 Gordonia-Alatamaha State Park

Location: In Reidsville.

Sites: 23 tent/RV sites with water and electricity, including 3 pull-throughs; maximum RV length 35 feet; dump station and comfort stations with flush toilets, showers, and coin laundry on-site.

Fee per night: $$$$.

Season: Year-round.

Management: Gordonia-Alatamaha State Park, (912) 557–7744. Reservations: (800) 864–7275.

Finding the campground: From downtown Reidsville go west on U.S. Route 280 for 0.5 mile to the park entrance.

About the campground: This park caters to all ages of campers, offering a nine-hole golf course for the big people and miniature golf for the little duffers. Picnic sites abound, and the twelve-acre lake offers some pretty good fishing. Boat rentals are available at the park. The park also has a swimming pool, tennis courts, and an observation deck overlooking a beaver dam and lodge.

20 Magnolia Springs State Park

Location: About 5 miles north of Millen.

Sites: 26 tent/RV sites with water and electricity, including 5 pull-throughs; maximum RV length 50 feet; dump station and comfort station with flush toilets, showers, and coin laundry on-site. Group camping area available by reservation only.

Fee per night: $$$$.

Season: Year-round.

Management: Magnolia Springs State Park, (912) 982–1660. Reservations: (800) 864–7275.

Finding the campground: From Millen go north on U.S. Route 25 for 5 miles to the park entrance.

About the campground: Named after the natural spring that graces the property, this park offers lots of ways to enjoy the water and natural surroundings. A fishing dock and boat rentals make fishing easy. A swimming pool and three playgrounds keep younger campers cool and occupied. An aquarium and an interpretive boardwalk offer nature lovers a great opportunity to see more of the natural surroundings. Campsites are reasonably well spaced and decently wooded.

The Coastal Region

Georgia enjoys more than 100 miles of coastline along the Atlantic Ocean. The coastal region is a wonderful combination of breathtaking natural beauty, gentile southern hospitality and history, and modern growth and development. The coast is home to many of the oldest settlements in the state, and much of the early history of the coast and its people has been well preserved and documented. Take some time to explore the historic sites and educational opportunities available. Within the same region lies a wonderland of natural beauty, including one of the largest swamps in the United States and a coastal habitat rich in wildlife. One trip to the region is not enough, and campers will find themselves returning again and again to sample the rich flavor of the Georgia coast.

Okefenokee Swamp Area

1 Stephen C. Foster State Park

Location: About 18 miles northeast of Fargo.
Sites: 65 tent/RV sites with water and electricity, including 8 pull-throughs; maximum RV length 60 feet; dump station and comfort stations with flush toilets, showers, and coin laundry on-site. Group camping area available by reservation only.
Fee per night: $$$$.
Season: Year-round.
Management: Stephen C. Foster State Park, (912) 637–5274. Reservations: (800) 864–7275.
Finding the campground: From Fargo go south on U.S. Route 441 for 1 mile. Turn left (northeast) onto GA 177 and travel 18 miles. The road ends at the park entrance.

About the campground: This park is one of the most popular entrances to the fabled Okefenokee Swamp. Park visitors will be fascinated by the surrounding ecology. An excellent interpretive center offers campers insight into the area's history and natural diversity, and an elevated boardwalk that treks 0.5 mile into the swamp offers lots of opportunities for spotting wildlife. Be sure to take one of the guided boat trips for even more incredible sights; the more adventurous can rent boats or canoes at the park to go fishing or just explore. The campsites are nicely wooded and spaced, and reasonably well shaded.

2 Laura S. Walker State Park

Location: About 9 miles southeast of Waycross.
Sites: 44 tent/RV sites with water and electricity; maximum RV length 40 feet; dump station and comfort stations with flush toilets, showers, and coin laundry

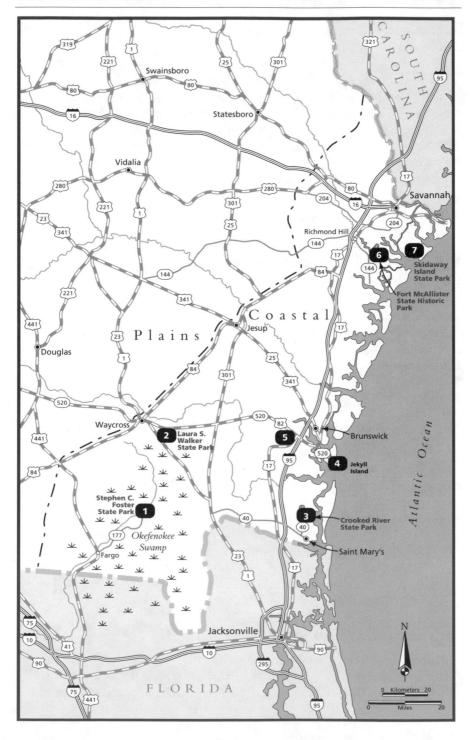

	Group sites	RV	Sites	Max. RV length	Hookups	Toilets	Showers	Coin laundry	Water	Dump	Pets	Handicap access	Recreation	Fee	Season	Can reserve	Stay limit
1 Stephen C. Foster SP	Y	Y	65	60	WE	F	Y	Y	Y	Y	Y	Y	BFH	$$$$		Y	14
2 Laura S. Walker SP	Y	Y	44	40	WE	F	Y	Y	Y	Y	Y	Y	BFGHS	$$$$		Y	14
3 Crooked River SP	Y	Y	60	40	WE	F	Y	Y	Y	Y	Y	Y	BFLS	$$$$		Y	14
4 Jekyll Island	N	Y	158	40	WES	F	Y	Y	Y	Y	Y	N	FHS	$$$$		Y	14
5 Blythe Island	N	Y	70	40	WES	F	Y	Y	Y	Y	Y	Y	BFLS	$$$$		Y	14
6 Fort McAllister SHP	Y	Y	65	50	WE	F	Y	Y	Y	Y	Y	Y	BFHL	$$$$		Y	14
7 Skidaway Island SP	Y	Y	88	40	WE	F	Y	Y	Y	Y	Y	Y	FH	$$$$		Y	14

Hookups: W = Water E = Electric S = Sewer **Toilets:** F = Flush V = Vault **Recreation:** B = Boating F = Fishing G = Golf H = Hiking L = Boat Launch M = Mountain Biking O = Off-Road Vehicles R = Horseback Riding S = Swimming T = Tennis **Fee:** $, less than $10; $$, $10–$15; $$$, $16–$20; $$$$, more than $20. **Maximum RV length** given in feet. **Stay limit** given in days. If no entry under **Season**, campgound is open all year. If no entry under **Fee**, camping is free.

on-site. Group camping area available by reservation only.

Fee per night: $$$$.

Season: Year-round.

Management: Laura S. Walker State Park, (912) 287–4900. Reservations: (800) 864–7275.

Finding the campground: From Waycross go east on U.S. Route 82/GA 520 for 8 miles. Turn right (south) onto GA 177, and travel 2 miles to the park entrance.

About the campground: This park offers another look at the unique ecosystem that is the Okefenokee Swamp. The park is located within a few miles of the north end of the swamp and is home to many diverse species of plant and animal life, some visible along the park's nature trail. For the recreation-minded, the park also has an eighteen-hole golf course, fishing, swimming, and water skiing on the 120-acre lake, and boat rentals. Kids are not forgotten either, with playgrounds for the little'uns. Take time to visit the nearby attractions that tell the colorful story of the area's past. You'll find excellent information in the park office.

Saint Mary's, Brunswick, and Jekyll Island

3 Crooked River State Park

Location: About 7 miles north of Saint Mary's.

Sites: 60 tent/RV sites with water and electricity, including 15 pull-throughs; maximum RV length 40 feet; dump station and comfort stations with flush toilets, showers, and coin laundry on-site. Group camping area available by reservation only.

Fee per night: $$$$.

Season: Year-round.
Management: Crooked River State Park, (912) 882–5256. Reservations: (800) 864–7275.
Finding the campground: From the intersection of GA 40 and Spur 40 in Saint Mary's, go north on Spur 40 for 4 miles to the park entrance.

About the campground: This park, named after the river that the park overlooks, is one of the few places for campers to enjoy the coastal inland waterways and quiet beauty of the region. Anglers enjoy the river, and the boat ramps provide access for campers and locals alike. A swimming pool, playgrounds, and miniature golf ensure entertainment for most ages. The campsites are well spaced, and some surround the open playground located in the middle of the campground. Outlying sites are tucked away more into the woods and offer more privacy.

4 Jekyll Island Campground

Location: Jekyll Island.
Sites: 158 tent/RV sites with water and electricity, including 98 with sewer hookups and 26 pull-throughs; maximum RV length 40 feet; dump station and comfort stations with flush toilets, showers, and laundry on-site.
Fee per night: $$$$.
Season: Year-round.
Management: Jekyll Island Campground, (912) 635–3021.
Finding the campground: The campground is located on North Beachview Drive on the north end of the island.

About the campground: Jekyll Island was once a millionaire's winter playground, and one can still tour the "cottages" those folks enjoyed. The island enjoys miles of beautiful beach; most of it is open to the public. Near the campground are some old tabby ruins of plantation buildings. The entire island is accessible by bicycle, with excellent hiking and biking paths to most parts. There's also fishing to keep everyone entertained. The campsites are close together and fairly wooded but don't offer much in the way of privacy. If you want to enjoy Jekyll Island's beauty and history, the campground offers a great alternative to the sometimes pricey hotels and motels that most visitors use.

5 Blythe Island Regional Park

Location: About 2.5 miles west of Brunswick.
Sites: 70 tent/RV sites with water and electricity, including 40 with sewer and 14 pull-throughs; maximum RV length 40 feet; dump station and comfort stations with flush toilets, showers, and coin laundry on-site.
Fee per night: $$$$.
Season: Year-round.

Management: Blythe Island Regional Park, (800) 343–7855.
Finding the campground: From the intersection of I–95 and U.S. Route 17 (exit 29) west of Brunswick, go west on U.S. Route 17 for 0.5 mile. Turn right (north) onto GA 303, and travel 3 miles to the park entrance.

About the campground: The area's excellent fishing is a major draw for this park, and locals use the facilities to access the many inland waterways that lace the area. The park feels nicely isolated even though it is relatively close to Brunswick. Sites are nicely wooded and spaced well, and campers will enjoy the privacy that the campground's location within the park offers. Facilities include boat ramps, a swimming area, fishing docks, a marina, and boat rentals. There are horseshoe pits in the campground and playgrounds to keep the little ones occupied.

Savannah Area

6 Fort McAllister State Historic Park

Location: About 7.5 miles southeast of Richmond Hill.
Sites: 65 tent/RV sites with water and electricity, including 55 pull-throughs; maximum RV length 50 feet; dump station and comfort stations with flush toilets, showers, and coin laundry on-site. Group camping area available by reservation only.
Fee per night: $$$$.
Season: Year-round.
Management: Fort McAllister State Historic Park, (912) 727–2339. Reservations: (800) 864–7275.
Finding the campground: From Richmond Hill go southeast on GA 144 for 4.4 miles. Turn left (east) onto Spur 144, and travel 3.5 miles to the park entrance.

About the campground: The focus of this historic area is the well-preserved confederate fort built to protect the Great Ogeechee River during the Civil War. The interpretive self-guided tour around the fort is fascinating, and the surroundings are beautiful, with towering live oaks and great views of the river and marshes from all directions. The campground is located on a peninsula out in the marsh and is surrounded completely—except for the entrance road—by salt- and freshwater marsh. Fishing docks and boat ramps offer lots of water access for anglers, and wildlife lovers will enjoy the many opportunities for spotting birds while hiking through the surrounding marshlands. Sites are nicely spaced. They are not particularly wooded, but offer lots of privacy. The campground is the only facility on the peninsula and offers a great sense of isolation from the rest of the world.

7 Skidaway Island State Park

Location: About 6 miles southeast of Savannah.
Sites: 88 tent/RV sites with water and electricity, all pull-throughs; maximum RV length 40 feet; dump station and comfort stations with flush toilets, showers, and

coin laundry on-site. Group camping area available by reservation only.
Fee per night: $$$$.
Season: Year-round.
Management: Skidaway Island State Park, (912) 598–2300. Reservations: (800) 864–7275.
Finding the campground: From the intersection of GA 204 and GA Spur 204 south of Savannah, go southeast on GA Spur 204 for 6.6 miles to the park entrance.

About the campground: The surroundings of this park are beautiful. The park lies on the intracoastal waterway, which has good fishing, with salt- and freshwater marshes along the edges of the park. The campsites are nicely wooded and well spaced and offer as much or as little privacy as campers wish. The two nature trails in the park give campers an opportunity to tour the local ecosystem and get a feel for what the area was like in the past. The surrounding development makes it a little more difficult to feel like you're "away from it all" at this park, especially at night, when the surrounding lights and traffic noise remind one of how populous the area is. Still, the park makes for a pleasant place to spend a few nights and offers one of the few places campers can stay and be convenient to the rich history of nearby Savannah.

Other Areas

The purpose of this book is to list campgrounds that are accessible by car. If your camping tastes are a little more adventurous, check with the U.S.D.A. Forest Service. They maintain several camping areas in wilderness areas and backcountry sites that are only accessible on foot or horseback. The Len Foote Hike-In Lodge at Amicolola Falls State Park is a neat alternative to self-supported hike-in camping; you'll find lots of creature comforts at the lodge, but you'll hike 5 miles or so to get there.

Talullah Falls State Park is also in the process of adding walk-in sleeping shelters. Other state parks are taking a close look at such ideas, where appropriate.

The Boy Scouts of America and Girl Scouts of America have several group camping areas in the state that are for the use of these and other groups. The Cumberland Island National Wildlife Refuge offers campers the opportunity to access the island via ferry; there are no vehicles allowed on the island except for official use. There are two campgrounds on the island, one more developed than the other. Camping here is a memorable experience and one of the last opportunities to experience the Georgia coast as it used to be. The state of Georgia and its various land management agencies are somewhat proactive in attempting to acquire public lands for recreational use in the face of such widespread development. I hope that the success of those efforts will warrant an update to this book to add new facilities and campgrounds.

For More Information

Georgia State Parks and Historic Sites
205 Butler Street
1352 Floyd Tower East
Atlanta, GA 30334
(800) 864–7275 (reservations)
(770) 389–7275 (in metro Atlanta)
www.gastateparks.org/

U.S. Army Corps of Engineers, Savannah District
P.O. Box 889
Savannah, GA 31402-0889
(912) 652–5822
www.sas.usace.army.mil/lakes/

U.S. Army Corps of Engineers, Mobile District
P.O. Box 2288
Mobile, AL 36628-0001
(800) 543–2021
www.sam.usace.army.mil/

Chattahoochee-Oconee National Forests
Forest Supervisor's Office
1755 Cleveland Highway
Gainesville, GA 30501
(770) 297–3000
www.fs.fed.us/conf/welcome.htm

Georgia Power Company
241 Ralph McGill Boulevard Northeast
Atlanta, GA 30308
(888) 472–5253
www.georgiapower.com/gpclake

The National Recreation Reservation Service (NRRS) is a joint venture of the U.S.
Forest Service and the U.S. Army Corps of Engineers. It offers a reservation service
for facilities managed by these agencies.
NRRS
(877) 444–6777
www.reserveusa.com/about/

Cumberland Island National Seashore
P.O. Box 806
St. Mary's, GA 31558
(912) 882–4336

There are several other Web-based reservation services available as well. Use your search engine to locate them; addresses and/or URLs tend to change more often than with the aforementioned agencies.

Index

About the Author

Alex Nutt is a lifelong resident of Georgia and a Georgian at heart as well. He has traveled throughout the state since childhood and has a fond appreciation for Georgia's diverse history, natural resources, and culture. He has worked as a volunteer with several land-management agencies in the state and spends as much of his free time as possible on one of his favorite causes: land access and public recreation. Besides enjoying camping and other outdoor activities, Alex is also an avid mountain biker and the author of Falcon's *Mountain Biking Georgia*. He currently lives with his family in middle Georgia, the "heart of the state."

What's So Special about Unspoiled, Natural Places?

Beauty   Solitude   Wildness   Freedom   Quiet   Adventure
Serenity   Inspiration   Wonder   Excitement
Relaxation   Challenge

There's a lot to love about our treasured public lands, and the reasons are different for each of us. Whatever your reasons are, the national **Leave No Trace** education program will help you discover special outdoor places, enjoy them, and preserve them—today and for those who follow. By practicing and passing along these simple principles, you can help protect the special places you love from being loved to death.

The Principles of Leave No Trace

- ❦ Plan ahead and prepare
- ❦ Travel and camp on durable surfaces
- ❦ Dispose of waste properly
- ❦ Leave what you find
- ❦ Minimize campfire impacts
- ❦ Respect wildlife
- ❦ Be considerate of other visitors

Leave No Trace is a national nonprofit organization dedicated to teaching responsible outdoor recreation skills and ethics to everyone who enjoys spending time outdoors.

To learn more or to become a member, please visit us at www.LNT.org or call (800) 332-4100.

Leave No Trace, P.O. Box 997, Boulder, CO 80306